I0020735

eZ Publish 4: Enterprise Web Sites Step-by-Step

Master eZ Publish's flexible web development for the enterprise

Francesco Fullone

Francesco Trucchia

BIRMINGHAM - MUMBAI

eZ Publish 4: Enterprise Web Sites Step-by-Step

Copyright © 2009 Packt Publishing

All rights reserved. No part of this book may be reproduced, stored in a retrieval system, or transmitted in any form or by any means, without the prior written permission of the publisher, except in the case of brief quotations embedded in critical articles or reviews.

Every effort has been made in the preparation of this book to ensure the accuracy of the information presented. However, the information contained in this book is sold without warranty, either express or implied. Neither the authors, Packt Publishing, nor its dealers or distributors will be held liable for any damages caused or alleged to be caused directly or indirectly by this book.

Packt Publishing has endeavored to provide trademark information about all the companies and products mentioned in this book by the appropriate use of capitals. However, Packt Publishing cannot guarantee the accuracy of this information.

First published: October 2009

Production Reference: 1151009

Published by Packt Publishing Ltd.
32 Lincoln Road
Olton
Birmingham, B27 6PA, UK.

ISBN 978-1-904811-64-0

www.packtpub.com

Cover Image by Vinayak Chittar (vinayak.chittar@gmail.com)

Credits

Authors
Francesco Fullone
Francesco Trucchia

Reviewer
Maxime Thomas

Acquisition Editor
James Lumsden

Development Editor
Amey Kanse

Technical Editor
Bhupali Khule

Copy Editor
Sneha Kulkarni

Indexer
Monica Ajmera

Editorial Team Leader
Akshara Aware

Project Team Leader
Lata Basantani

Project Coordinator
Rajashree Hamine

Proofreader
Dirk Manuel

Graphics
Nilesh R Mohite

Production Coordinator
Dolly Dasilva

Cover Work
Dolly Dasilva

About the Authors

Francesco Fullone is a geek who, in his spare time, acts as the founder and the CEO of Ideato, a Web 2.0 company based in Italy. He is a senior consultant, skilled in Agile methods and any kind of PHP development.

Francesco is also the president of the Italian PHP User Group (GrUSP) and an evangelist on open source software and PHP technologies. You can meet him in Italy at one of the tech conferences, where he usually participates as a speaker or a staff member.

Francesco would like to thank the Ideato family for the help given during the testing of the book's code, the Packt staff for their patience towards a new author and Diana, who supported him in this "adventure".

Francesco Trucchia, after taking a degree in computer science, worked for some years as a web engineer on small, medium, and large projects for some Italian companies.

He is now the co-founder and the CTO of Ideato, a PHP Italian company that is expert in web software development, systems integration, and Agile methods.

Francesco likes to develop with Agile methods. He has introduced these practices in Ideato for their software's lifecycle process, and has received a lot of positive feedback for it.

Francesco would like to thank his company, Ideato, that gave him the opportunity to write this book, all the Pack editorial staff, particularly Rajashree, Bhupali, Amey, and Sneha for their great patience, assistance, and professionalism, the eZ System company for the great work that they are doing to make eZ Publish the best Open Source CMS, his family and his fiancée Chiara who supported and encouraged him every day on writing this book.

About the Reviewer

Maxime Thomas has a degree in computer science from ESIAL University in Nancy, France. He worked for two years as a developer in a French company specializing in IT services, which has given him his web culture and has contributed to his knowledge of the basic rules of design for websites. For two years now, he's been responsible of the open source CMS offers at a major IT service company, mainly working with offers for the media sector. He has been certified in eZ Publish since 2007 and shares his ideas on his blog, which is available at `http://www.wascou.org/ wascou/Blogs/Maxime-THOMAS`.

I would like to thank the people with whom I can share information about eZ Publish: Xavier, Damien, and Benoit. I also would like to thank Vincent, who has changed my opinion on open source software, and eZ Publish in particular. Finally, I would like to thank Ana for her every day support.

Table of Contents

Preface   **1**

Chapter 1: Installing eZ Publish   **9**

What is eZ Publish?   **9**

  What is a CMF?   10

eZ Publish packages   **10**

  eZ Webin—the out of the box CMS   11

  eZ Flow—web publishing for news and media portals   11

Installation   **12**

  Hosting requirements   12

    Software required   12

    Hardware required   13

    PHP configuration   13

    Shared versus dedicated hosting   14

  eZ components   15

  Setting up   16

    Unpacking the installation   16

    Initializing the database   16

    Apache virtual host settings   17

    Image settings   20

    Cron jobs   20

    Configuration files   21

The setup wizard   **22**

  Welcome to eZ Publish   23

    System check   23

    Email settings   25

    Choose a database   26

    Database initialization   27

    Language support   28

    Site packages   29

    Site access configuration   32

    Site details   33

    Site security   34

Site registration	35
Finished	36
Summary	**36**
Chapter 2: Creating Our Siteaccesses	**37**
What is the siteaccess system?	**37**
Siteaccess folder structure	39
Enterprise siteaccess schema	41
Creating siteaccesses for dev and staging	41
Creating symbolic links	42
Configuring the database parameters	43
Creating multilingual siteaccesses	**44**
Copying the configuration file	44
Editing ini files for locale components	44
Selecting a siteaccess using host or URI-based matching	**46**
URI	46
Setting the default siteaccess	46
Host	47
Summary	**47**
Chapter 3: Defining and Creating Content Classes	**49**
Managing the content	**49**
Separation of content and design	50
Content structure in eZ Publish	50
Object-oriented content	50
eZ Publish content classes	**52**
Class attributes	52
Content class management	54
Content class structure	56
Packt Media Site's content class	**58**
Creating the profile content class	59
Extending the Article class	63
The other content classes	65
Summary	**65**
Chapter 4: Creating Content Structure	**67**
Understanding the backend	**68**
Content structure	69
The secondary menu	70
The content area	71
The content tree	**75**
The "Issue archive" section	75
Editing an object	76
Adding more folders	82
The staff section	83

Creating an article   85
    Publish and Unpublish date   86
    Enabling comments   86
The feedback form   87
Other sections   88
Summary   **88**

Chapter 5: Creating an Extension   **89**
What is an extension?   **89**
Extension type   90
The directory structure of an extension   90
Build the extension   **91**
Settings extension   92
Design an extension   92
Template operator extension   94
Translations extension   94
Activating an extension   **96**
Manual activation   96
Backend activation   97
Design activation   98
Extension portability   **98**
Content class package   99
Extension packages   103
Business with extensions   **105**
Summary   **105**

Chapter 6: Creating a Design   **107**
eZ Publish templating   **107**
Templating   107
The templating markup   108
    Control structure operators   108
    Fetch functions   109
    Generic template functions and operators   110
Creating a new design   **113**
The homepage   114
Issue page   115
The issue archive   116
The staff profile page   116
eZ Webin   **117**
Overriding the standard page layout   118
    Section for our project   118
    Creating a new section   118
    Setting up the section permission access   120

Customizing the page layout	123
CSS editing	124
Creating a new style package	124
Summary	**128**
Chapter 7: Template Content Class	**129**
Introduction to the content template	**129**
The override system	**130**
Creating a template override	130
Creating a template override from a graphic interface	131
Creating a template override manually	134
Profile class	135
Folder class for the issue year archive	136
Folder class for issue	136
Folder class for the issue archive section	138
Article class	138
Frontpage embed object	139
Creating our custom template file	140
Customizing our class templates	**140**
Staff profile template	140
Line template	140
Full template	143
Embed template	146
Issue template	146
Line template	146
Full template	148
Thumb template	151
Embed template	152
Issue archive template	152
Full template	153
Embed template	155
Issue year template	155
Full template	156
Issue article template	157
Line template	157
Full template	159
Embed template	165
Summary	**166**
Chapter 8: Adding Community Forums	**167**
The magazine's forum	**168**
Adding the Forum	168
Creating a sticky post	170
Forum access control list	170
Creating the Private forums section	171

Creating the magazine's blog   **173**
  Adding the blog   174
Set up the feeds   **175**
  Creating the blog feed   176
  Creating the forum feed   180
Summary   **181**

Chapter 9: Internationalization and Localization   **183**
A multilingual site   **183**
  Internationalization   184
  Localization   184
  Locale identifiers   184
    Creating a new locale file   184
Multi-language site management   **186**
  Class attribute translations   187
    Class default language   190
  Content translation   190
  URL translation   191
Multilingual extensions   **192**
  The extension folder structure   193
  The extension siteaccess   193
  The template strings   194
Summary   **194**

Chapter 10: Creating Roles and Privileges   **195**
Policies, roles, and groups   **195**
  Policies   196
  Roles   196
    Applying a role   196
  User groups   197
eZ Publish user management   **197**
  User accounts   198
  Creating a new user   199
    Extending eZ Publish user classes   202
  Managing a user   202
    Disabling a user   202
    Deleting a user   203
  The eZ Webin predefined groups   204
Some steps into the workflows   **204**
  The default workflow events   205
    Approve   205
    Wait until date   205
    Multiplexer   205

Simple Shipping	205
Payment Gateway	206
Creating a notification workflow	206
Summary	**211**
Chapter 11: Cache Configuration	**213**
Caching system	**213**
Template cache	214
eZ Webin cache block	215
Compiling a template	216
Template optimization	216
View cache	216
Enabling/Disabling the cache by context	217
Clearing the view cache	218
Smart cache	220
Default caching settings	**223**
Advanced eZ Publish caching system	**224**
Advanced settings	224
Override cache	224
Pre-generation cache	224
Translation cache	225
Role cache	225
Static cache	225
Opcode cache	226
Proxy and HTTP Accelerator	227
Customize cache settings to speed up the performance	**228**
What not to do in a template	**229**
Summary	**230**
Chapter 12: Deployment	**231**
Environments	**231**
Development environment	232
Staging environment	232
Production environment	232
Preparing the production server	233
Deploying an eZ Publish site	**233**
eZ Deploy	234
Creating the automatic tests	234
Installing the Selenium IDE	236
Recording a session	236
Customizing tests	238
Configuring the staging and production siteaccesses	240
Deploying the database	241
Deploying the code	241
Configuring the extension	241

Excluding files from deploy 242
Starting the synchronization 243
Checking the validity 243
Quality assurance 245
Deploying to the production server 245
Summary **245**
Appendix A: APC Installation and Optimization **247**
APC tuning for eZ Publish **247**
Opcode Cache 247
How does it work? 248
Installing APC 248
Installing from sources 249
PECL installation 249
APC configuration 249
APC GUI 251
Performance 252
Appendix B: Advance Debugging **253**
Code debugger 253
Debug template operators 254
Templating debug 255
Appendix C: eZ Publish's Best Extensions **259**
eZ Xajax **259**
Star Rating **259**
eZ Publish OE **260**
eZ JSCore **260**
Google Sitemaps **260**
eZ Deploy **261**
Data Import **261**
Index **263**

Preface

Welcome to our book on building websites with eZ Publish. Before starting to learn how to use it to create a site, let's take a short moment to better understand the overall context of content management on the internet.

In recent years, we have seen the evolution of the Content Management Systems, or CMSes. This kind of software from a simple set of tools for managing text and pages of a website, has had to adapt and evolve to become more flexible. Nowadays, CMSes need to be extensible, and use plugins or vertical modules to cater for different needs.

The concept of a web page has moved from being a mere graphical representation of information to a point where we can decouple the content from the presentation. In turn, we can also decouple content from its publication media. Today, a single item of content can be represented in boundless ways (for example, through the use of Cascading Style Sheets, or CSS), and can be made accessible from almost any device, through such things as RSS, Microformat, and so on.

Disciplines such as IA (Information Architecture) have made great strides in determining how content should be managed. New information structures have been developed across the years, from the simple and limited hierarchy of categories, to multi-structured and more complex data organizations now used in any context.

In short, the Internet has become a 360-degree communication platform, which increasingly uses various media in a single context. But the internet is also all about content, which can be represented in a lot of different ways.

This is a big problem for developers who have to create and manage sites. These new concepts have introduced new challenges for the management of websites.

In fact, the rigidity of managing information, as characterized by the old CMS generation, has led many developers to seek new solutions—solutions that are customizable according to the needs of the moment.

eZ Publish

eZ Publish was born for new media and enterprise content publishing. This product can be used by all levels of developer to build corporate websites, intranets, web shops, and media portals. eZ Publish is 100% open-source, available either as a free download or as an enterprise solution (as eZ Publish Premium with support, guarantees, and maintenance for companies that need advanced help).

In the first year of its life, eZ Publish moved from a Content Management System approach to a Content Management Framework approach. A Content Management Framework, or CMF, can be defined as an application programming interface for creating a customized Content Management System.

In this book, we will be building an enterprise website with eZ Publish. eZ Publish is well-suited to a project like this due to its structured content model and versioning capabilities, as well as pre-built functionality that ensures rapid and professional deployment with minimal fuss.

eZ Publish has some key features:

- It comes with a number of ready-to-use website packages.
- It has lots of predefined, solid, and useful functionality.
- It is flexible. Any behavior or components can be extended or overwritten.

Introducing the project

This book will focus on the delivery of a standards-based enterprise website for a magazine adopting eZ Publish for the first time. The book will feature a single magazine project from installation through to completion and deployment of the eZ Publish website.

The project in detail

This book is divided into three main areas: set-up, creating content, and managing it. We won't follow a linear approach but instead will try to see what we need in any given area to accomplish our tasks and then, chapter by chapter, we will drill down into concepts when needed.

- Set-up: We perform a complete eZ Publish installation on a LAMP platform, where we will see how to configure the environment, and how to install the standard layout that we will customize in the other chapters.

- Creating the content types and structures: We will define the content and the structures that we will use for our magazine site. We will also create custom content for managing some deeper information.

- Managing content: eZ Publish allows us to do a lot of things with content and layout. In this area we will customize one of the standard and flexible eZ Publish templates that comes bundled with the Content Management Framework, in order to fulfill our needs. We will also set up some useful services, such as internationalization, site subscription, and a forum for creating interaction with the users. And, obviously, we will also create our site pages.

What this book covers

Chapter 1, Installing eZ Publish: This chapter will look at the processes involved in installing eZ Publish for the magazine project, including hosting requirements. The choices that need to be made during installation will also be covered.

Chapter 2, Creating Our Site Accesses: What are siteaccesses? When we work on a customer site it is useful to have different environments available to show your customer what we are doing. In this chapter, we'll create some simple site access rules to manage these areas. We will also take a deeper look at what site accesses are, and how they work.

Chapter 3, Defining and Creating Content Classes: This chapter will introduce us to the standard content classes of eZ Publish. We will also learn to create the required classes, for the additional structured content, as defined by the project.

Chapter 4, Creating Content Structure: This chapter will look at creating the default content structure for the magazine, as well as adding some initial content, so that we can see the structure and layout of various default content classes. We'll also introduce the eZ Publish backend and its functionality.

Chapter 5 Creating an Extension: We will create an extension to hold all of our customizations for this project, which is much better than working in the standard folders and will help us in any future system upgrade.

Chapter 6 Template Design: In this chapter, we will see how to apply a template to a single content or to a node folder. We will also take a look at the template overrides, and creating a design extension.

Chapter 7 Template Content Classes: Custom templates for content approval and checkout processes are important concepts in many eZ Publish undertakings, and will be featured in this chapter. We will also create a custom template for both a standard class and a custom class.

Chapter 8 Adding Community Forums: In this chapter we'll take a look at the built-in forums available through the **ezwebin** packages. We will implement these content classes and templates, and then work on them further, adding functionality that was not previously included in eZ Publish 4.0, but which will be useful to the magazine.

Chapter 9 Internationalization and localization: This chapter provides a brief overview of the internationalization capabilities of eZ Publish. We will implement some additional language translations for our customers who may be visiting and looking to enroll at the magazine.

Chapter 10 Creating Roles and Privileges: After all of this defining and creating, we need to actually get useful content into the system. There are a number of approaches to do so, and this chapter will cover the main ones in detail, with a short discussion on other methods.

Chapter 11 Cache configuration: The cache system is one of the most important subsystems of eZ Publish. In this chapter, we will explain how to use it and how to customize it for our needs.

Chapter 12 Deployment: The deployment chapter investigates the processes associated with deploying our development site to production.

Appendix A, APC Tuning for eZ Publish: eZ Publish, to publish the web pages, has to elaborate a lot of data. This work, in some cases, can be a CPU-eater and may slow down the response of the server. For this reason, we will learn how to install and use an opcode cache system, such as APC.

Appendix B, Advance Debugging: During the development of the eZ Publish site, it is very important to receive immediate feedback about what we are doing. We will learn how to enable and use the code debugger and the template debugger that are included in the CMF.

Appendix C, eZ Publish Extensions: We will introduce some of the best extensions developed by the eZ Publish community.

What you need for this book

Unless otherwise stated, the environment used in the examples, and referred to throughout the book, is a LAMP platform with PHP 5.2.x, MySQL 5.x and eZ Publish 4.0.1. We'll use the shipped eZ webin template that eZ System offers bundled with the CMF.

Who this book is for

If you need to work on a site with a complex publishing workflow, or have to manage an enterprise level site and want to use eZ Publish from scratch and without requiring hardcore programming skills, this is the book you need.

You will learn how to install, manage and customize the eZ Publish platform. This book is for you if you are not a PHP-guru, and you don't want to study the eZ Publish core functionality.

In general, however, you'll get more out of the book if you know a little PHP, understand some concepts of Object Oriented Programming, and have a general familiarity with CMS concepts.

Conventions

In this book, you will find a number of styles of text that distinguish between different kinds of information. Here are some examples of these styles, and an explanation of their meaning.

Code words in text are shown as follows: "We can include other contexts through the use of the `include` directive."

A block of code will be set as follows:

```
<? /* #?ini charset="utf-8"?

[ExtensionSettings]
DesignExtensions[]=packtmedia

*/ ?>
```

When we wish to draw your attention to a particular part of a code block, the relevant lines or items will be shown in bold:

```
<?php /* #?ini charset="utf-8"?
...
[RegionalSettings]
TranslationExtensions[]=packtmedia
...
*/ ?>
```

Any command-line input or output is written as follows:

```
# cd /var/www/packtmediaproject
# cd extension/
# mkdir packtmedia
```

New terms and **important words** are shown in bold. Words that you see on the screen, in menus or dialog boxes for example, appear in our text like this: "Click on the **Setup** tab on top menu."

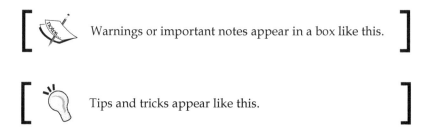

Warnings or important notes appear in a box like this.

Tips and tricks appear like this.

Reader feedback

Feedback from our readers is always welcome. Let us know what you think about this book—what you liked or may have disliked. Reader feedback is important for us to develop titles that you really get the most out of.

To send us general feedback, simply drop an email to feedback@packtpub.com, and mention the book title in the subject of your message.

If there is a book that you need and would like to see us publish, please send us a note in the **SUGGEST A TITLE** form on www.packtpub.com or email suggest@packtpub.com.

If there is a topic that you have expertise in and you are interested in either writing or contributing to a book, see our author guide on www.packtpub.com/authors.

Customer support

Now that you are the proud owner of a Packt book, we have a number of things to help you to get the most from your purchase.

Downloading the example code for the book

Visit http://www.packtpub.com/files/code/1640_Code.zip to directly
download the example code.

 The downloadable files contain instructions on how to use them.

Errata

Although we have taken every care to ensure the accuracy of our contents, mistakes
do happen. If you find a mistake in one of our books—maybe a mistake in text or
code—we would be grateful if you would report this to us. By doing so, you can save
other readers from frustration and help us to improve subsequent versions of this
book. If you find any errata, please report them by visiting http://www.packtpub.
com/support, selecting your book, clicking on the **let us know** link, and entering
the details of your errata. Once your errata are verified, your submission will be
accepted and the errata added to any list of existing errata. Any existing errata can be
viewed by selecting your title from http://www.packtpub.com/support.

Piracy

Piracy of copyright material on the Internet is an ongoing problem across all media.
At Packt, we take the protection of our copyright and licenses very seriously.
If you come across any illegal copies of our works in any form on the Internet,
please provide us with the location address or website name immediately so that
we can pursue a remedy.

Please contact us at copyright@packtpub.com with a link to the suspected
pirated material.

We appreciate your help in protecting our authors, and our ability to bring you
valuable content.

Questions

You can contact us at questions@packtpub.com if you are having a problem
with any aspect of the book, and we will do our best to address it.

1
Installing eZ Publish

Enterprise content management (ECM) is a set of technologies used to capture, store, preserve and deliver content and documents related to organizational processes.

This definition is taken from `http://en.wikipedia.org/wiki/Enterprise_content_management`.

In this chapter, we will introduce the eZ Publish software. We will then prepare the development server by downloading the software and creating a database, and we will follow the installation wizard to have eZ Publish running on our server.

What is eZ Publish?

eZ Publish is an *Enterprise Content Management System*. It helps to build corporate websites, intranets, web shops, and media portals. Moreover, eZ Publish is 100% open source, available either as a free download or as an enterprise solution—*eZ Publish Premium*—with support, guarantees, and maintenance.

This software is designed to be used by small, medium, and large companies. It provides a lot of advanced features that can be used, by default, to create professional and secure solutions.

The software allows websites to be fully extended and modified, and unlike other CMSes, it's a truly scalable system.

eZ Publish supports, out of the box, the following features:

- The management of users' roles
- The ability to assign roles and policies to different content categories or types
- Definition of workflow tasks for collaborative creation, often coupled with integrated event messaging
- The ability to track and manage multiple versions of a single instance of content
- The ability to import content from other sources (that is, an OpenOffice document)

eZ Publish is more than a simple CMS; it is a **Content Management Framework (CMF)**. This means that it is much more flexible, extendable, and reusable.

What is a CMF?

A *content management framework* is an Application Programming Interface (API) for creating a customized content management system.

The eZ Publish kernel is crafted on top of **eZ CMF**, a content management framework fully developed by eZ System. This framework makes the eZ Publish functionality stable, secure, and well engineered. And thanks to the CMF, it is possible to extend and personalize the CMS features to provide specific tasks or create mashups and integrations with other open source products, such as CRMs, financial software, or e-commerce platforms.

The most recent releases of eZ Publish also use **eZ Components**, a set of independent components that will eventually replace all of the core functionality of eZ CMF. With eZ Publish 4.0, it is possible to develop extensions using these components that give a powerful API for each use.

eZ Publish packages

As we have said in the preface, it is very important to understand that eZ Publish offers (as downloaded) three main features:

- It comes with a number of ready-to-use website packages
- It has lots of hardcoded, solid, and useful functionality
- It is flexible—behavior and components can be extended or overwritten

Website packages are designed by the eZ System to use the main engine to help users deploy different sites with different scopes: a community site, a static one, or an intranet application. The three main packages are **Plain Site, eZ Webin,** and **eZ Flow.**

Whereas the first one is only a skeleton, on top of which a developer can craft his or her own application, the other two allow developers to use a lot of functionality without touching an IDE.

eZ Webin—the out of the box CMS

eZ Webin is a package that contains all of the functionality required to build a complete Web 2.0 site. It is fully documented by eZ System, and this documentation can be found at `http://ez.no/doc/extensions/website_interface`. eZ Webin is very useful for creating a site from scratch.

To build our site, we will use this package in the next chapters, customizing the site wherever needed.

eZ Webin includes:

- Tag clouds
- Blogs
- Forums
- Events management
- Calendars

eZ Flow—web publishing for news and media portals

Vibrant sites are all about content flow—getting the most engaging and timely content streams onto the site's critical portal pages. Built on top of eZ Publish as a result of collaboration and experience with media customers, the eZ Flow extension (`http://ez.no/doc/extensions/ez_flow`) enables editors to build complex page layouts and pre-plan the publication schedule to ensure a constant flow of rich content. In short, eZ Flow brings modern portal management possibilities to eZ Publish.

eZ Flow is a web package that provides the following added functionalities:

- Layouts based on zones and blocks
- Custom layouts
- The ability to fetch content from different sources

- The ability to search, order, hide, and push content
- Scheduling of content flow
- Multiple block-specific templates
- Previews of portal pages
- An intuitive Flash player
- Embedded video advertisement
- Live video streaming and recording
- Ranking and related media
- Native integrations with ad servers
- Connectors for web analytics

Installation

Before we start using the CMS/F, we have to check if our system is ready for it. As our first task, we will have to see if the hosting requirements are fulfilled. Then we will configure the PHP interpreter according to eZ Publish's needs.

Hosting requirements

One of the most important things to understand is that hosting plays a very important role in managing eZ Publish. The minimum requirements for installing eZ Publish, in terms of both software and hardware, are discussed in the subsequent sections.

Software required

- Apache server 1.3 or 2 if 2.x is installed, then the **prefork** package is used.
- MySql Server 4.1 or higher
- PHP 5.1 – but PHP 5.2 is recommended, compiled as a module for Apache and **not installed as a CGI** (eZ Publish does not work well with PHP installed as a CGI)
- Support for the GD graphics libraries, if ImageMagick is not available
- Support for Apache mod_rewrite, if you want to use the friendly URL
- FTP access, but SFTP/SSH access is recommended
- The eZ Components library

Hardware required

The installation requires about 50 MB on your hard disk, but as always, the more space you reserve for the system the better. For a good system experience, we suggest some minimum values: at least 1GHz CPU and 512 MB of dedicated RAM.

PHP configuration

As with any other software application developed in PHP, eZ Publish also needs some configuration to better work with the interpreter. The most important is the one related to memory usage and timezone settings. Moreover, the same settings should be applied to both the command-line site and to the Apache (or IIS) module.

PHP memory limit issue

eZ Publish needs at least 64 MB (but 128 is preferred) in order to complete the **Setup Wizard**. If you are using PHP 5.2.0 or an earlier version, you'll have to increase the default `memory_limit` setting, which is located in the `php.ini` configuration file (don't forget to restart Apache after editing `php.ini`). Normal operation requires about 16 MB. However, it is highly recommended that you keep the 64 MB setting as eZ Publish consumes a lot more memory as soon as you re-index the search, execute upgrade scripts, and so on.

If you are using PHP 5.2.1 or later, there is no need to change the default `memory_limit` setting (it is set to 128 MB by default).

PHP timezone

You need to set the `date.timezone` value in the `php.ini` configuration file. If this setting is not specified, you will most likely receive error messages like "*It is not safe to rely on the system's timezone settings*" when running eZ Publish on PHP 5. The following example shows what the corresponding line in `php.ini` looks like:

```
date.timezone = <timezone>
```

Refer to the PHP documentation for the list of supported timezones. As before, don't forget to restart Apache after editing `php.ini`.

Shared versus dedicated hosting

One of the main questions to consider before using eZ Publish is whether to use shared or dedicated hosting. There is no simple answer because the choice depends on the type of site that you develop. You have to take note that the variables that affect the performance of the CMS are:

- Number of page views per unit of time
- Number of concurrent visits
- Complexity of the template
- Freshness of content
- Number of nodes

If the site that you want to develop is a showcase site for a company, with few pages and few visitors, then the minimum requirements we saw in the previous paragraph will be sufficient.

If you want to develop a great site for a media agency, such as the project we'll develop in the next chapters, a site with high freshness of content, with a respectable number of visitors per day (over 5,000 unique visitors), where we will add advanced features and the ability of users to add content, then the minimum requirements will increase to:

- Dedicated Hosting
- 1 GB RAM
- Linux OS
- At least 1GB of free disk space
- Cronjobs management
- SSH access
- The eZ components library

For medium-sized projects, you can also use a **Virtual Private Server** (**VPS**), but if the site receives a lot of visits and the CMS makes extensive use of a caching system, then the performance could be diminished because of slow I/O. As a rule of thumb, when possible, try to avoid using virtual disks if you plan to have a popular site.

eZ components

eZ Publish is an object-oriented application where each class definition is stored in a separate PHP source file. When eZ Publish is installed, all of the class definitions of the eZ Publish kernel will have their paths listed in the `autoload/ezp_kernel.php` file. In addition, the `autoload/ezp_extension.php` file will contain an array of paths for class definitions that are a part of the extensions that come with eZ Publish. These arrays will most likely need to be updated at some stage (for example, when you install new extensions or configure existing ones by using the **Setup | Extensions** part of the administration interface). Doing this requires eZ components version 2007.1.1 (or higher). In particular, you need to install the File and Base components (`ezcBase` and `ezcFile`). Otherwise, eZ Publish will not be able to update autoload arrays.

eZ components is an enterprise-ready, general purpose PHP components library, used for PHP application development. eZ components can be downloaded from `http://ezcomponents.org/download`. In the future, eZ components will be bundled with eZ Publish. Refer to `http://ezcomponents.org/docs/install` for information about how to install eZ components.

Starting from version 2008.1, the eZ components library requires PHP version 5.2.1 or higher.

There are three ways to make eZ components available for your PHP environment:

- Use the PEAR Installer for convenient installation via the command line
- Download eZ components, packaged in an archive
- Get the latest source from SVN

Installing eZ components by way of the PEAR Installer is highly recommended, as it is the most convenient and safest way. You can find all required documentation on how to do this at `http://www.ezcomponents.org/docs/install`.

If you are in a shared hosting environment, and it is impossible for you to install eZ components as PEAR, there is a trick to installing it.

First of all, you will have to download the latest version of the components from `http://www.ezcomponents.org/download`. Then you have to extract the archive to the eZ Publish root, and rename the folder `ezc`. Now, in the same directory, you have to create a file named `config.php`, and enter the following code in it:

```php
<?php
set_include_path( "./ezc:" . ini_get( "include_path" )
);
?>
```

Setting up

After setting up the system, we need to perform a series of other tasks, before installing eZ Publish, such as creating a database or configuring the Apache environment.

 All examples are written to be performed from a shell, under the Linux operating system. If you do not have a shell, you can still perform all of these tasks through the tools provided by your host.

Unpacking the installation

First of all, download the latest version of eZ Publish from `http://www.ez.no/download` (at the time of writing this book, the latest version is 4.0.1). Unzip the file that you downloaded, to your web root, and rename the folder with the name of the project.

For example:

```
# cd /var/www
# wget http://ez.no/content/download/242355/1643191/version/1/file/
ezpublish-4.0.1-gpl.tar.gz
# tar -xvfz ezpublish-4.0.1-gpl.tar.gz
# mv ezpublish-4.0.1 packtmediaproject
# cd packtmediaproject
```

 From now on, every time we refer to the **eZ Publish root,** we are talking about this directory (the directory to which we unzipped the CMS).

Initializing the database

Once you have unpacked the source code of eZ Publish, you must create a new database. It is important that the `charset` (character set) of the new database is `UTF-8` as this has been a mandatory requirement for a correct installation since version 4.0.

eZ Publish can use both MySQL and PostgreSQL. In this book, all of the examples refer to the former, but you are free to use the latter.

To create a new database, open a shell and use the following code, which shows how to set the character set:

```
# mysql -u root
Welcome to the MySQL monitor. Commands end with ; or \g.
Your MySQL connection id is 1
Server version: 5.0.67 MySQL Community Server (GPL)
Type 'help;' or '\h' for help. Type '\c' to clear the buffer.
mysql> CREATE DATABASE packtmediaproject CHARACTER SET = 'utf8';
```

Now create a separate user called packuser who owns all rights to manage the database, and who can access the database only from localhost. You'll use this user in the eZ Publish configuration files.

```
mysql> GRANT ALL ON packtmediaproject.* TO 'packtuser'@'localhost'
  IDENTIFIED BY 'packtpwd';
Query OK, 1 row affected (0.00 sec)
mysql> FLUSH PRIVILEGES;
Query OK, 1 row affected (0.00 sec)
```

Apache virtual host settings

A virtual host setup is needed by eZ Publish only when configured to use the host access method, which is the suggested method.

When using virtual hosts, it is possible to have several sites running on the same server. The sites are usually differentiated by the name under which they are accessed. Apache will look for a specified set of domains and use different configuration settings based on the domain that is accessed.

Virtual hosts are usually defined at the end of the httpd.conf file, which is the main configuration file for Apache, and is placed on Debian-based distribution in /etc/apache2/conf. Adding a virtual host for eZ Publish can be done by copying the following lines and replacing the text encapsulated by the square brackets with real values.

Please refer to the following code for a real-life example of using virtual hosts.

```
NameVirtualHost [IP_ADDRESS]
<VirtualHost [IP_ADDRESS]:[PORT]>
    <Directory [PATH_TO_EZPUBLISH]>
        Options FollowSymLinks
        AllowOverride None
    </Directory>
    <IfModule mod_php5.c>
        php_admin_flag safe_mode Off
        php_admin_value register_globals 0
        php_value magic_quotes_gpc 0
        php_value magic_quotes_runtime 0
        php_value allow_call_time_pass_reference 0
    </IfModule>
    DirectoryIndex index.php
    <IfModule mod_rewrite.c>
        RewriteEngine On
        RewriteRule content/treemenu/? /index_treemenu.php [L]
        Rewriterule ^/var/storage/.* - [L]
        Rewriterule ^/var/[^/]+/storage/.* - [L]
        RewriteRule ^/var/cache/texttoimage/.* - [L]
        Rewriterule ^/var/[^/]+/cache/texttoimage/.* - [L]
        Rewriterule ^/design/[^/]+/(stylesheets|images|javascript)/.* -
        [L]
        Rewriterule ^/share/icons/.* - [L]
        Rewriterule ^/extension/[^/]+/design/[^/]+/(stylesheets|images|
            javascripts?)/.* - [L]
        Rewriterule ^/packages/styles/.+/
          (stylesheets|images|javascript)/[^/]+/.* - [L]
        RewriteRule ^/packages/styles/.+/thumbnail/.* - [L]
        RewriteRule ^/favicon\.ico - [L]
        RewriteRule ^/robots\.txt - [L]
        # Uncomment the following lines when using popup style debug.
        # RewriteRule ^/var/cache/debug\.html.* - [L]
        # RewriteRule ^/var/[^/]+/cache/debug\.html.* - [L]
        RewriteRule .* /index.php
    </IfModule>
    DocumentRoot [PATH_TO_EZPUBLISH]
    ServerName [SERVER_NAME]
    ServerAlias [SERVER_ALIAS]
</VirtualHost>
```

The following table explains the variables as referred to in the code above:

Variable	Description	Project value
[IP_ADDRESS]	The IP address of the virtual host. Apache allows the use of a wildcards here ("*").	localhost
[PORT]	The port on which the web server listens for incoming requests. This is an optional setting. The default port is 80. The combination of an IP address and a port is often referred to as a socket. Apache allows the use of a wildcards here ("*").	*
[PATH_TO_EZPUBLISH]	Path to the directory that contains eZ Publish. This must be the full path.	/var/www/packtmediaproject
[SERVER_NAME]	The host or the IP address that Apache should look for. If a match is found, the virtual host settings will be used.	packtmediaproject
[SERVER_ALIAS]	Additional hosts/IP addresses that Apache should look for. If a match is found, the virtual host settings will be used.	

 Please note that the mod_rewrite module must be enabled in httpd.conf in order to use the Rewrite Rules.

The NameVirtualHost setting might already exist in the default configuration. Defining a new one will result in a conflict. If Apache reports errors such as *"NameVirtualHost [IP_ADDRESS] has no VirtualHosts"* or *"Mixing * ports and non-* ports with a NameVirtualHost address is not supported"*, try skipping the NameVirtualHost line. For more information about the NameVirtualHost directive, see: http://httpd.apache.org/docs/1.3/mod/core.html#namevirtualhost.

If the ServerName is not a registered domain, you will need to add the record to the file /etc/hosts, so that the system DNS can resolve it.

Open the file /etc/hosts and insert the following code at the end of file:

```
127.0.0.1 packtmediaproject
```

Image settings

In order to scale, convert, or modify images, eZ Publish needs to make use of an image conversion system. Either of the following software packages (both are free) can be used:

- GD2 (comes with PHP)
- ImageMagick (`http://www.imagemagick.org`)

ImageMagick supports more formats than GD2 and usually produces better results (better scaling, and much more). The setup wizard will automatically detect the pre-installed image conversion system(s).

The installation and setup of required software solutions (outlined above) is far beyond the scope of this document. Please refer to the eZ Publish homepage and the relevant documentation for the different software solutions.

Cron jobs

Some features of eZ Publish depend on the maintenance script that takes care of various tasks behind the scenes. This script is located in the root of the eZ Publish directory and should be executed at regular intervals. The script is called `runcronjobs.php`. Among other things, it processes workflows, checks and validates URLs, sends out notification emails, and so on. Although eZ Publish works without a periodic execution of `runcronjobs.php`, it is still recommended that you have it running in the background. Some features, for example the notification system, will not work if the script is not running.

The most common practice is to instruct the operating system to automatically run the script every 30-60 minutes. However, some tasks should be executed more frequently than others, and thus it is a good idea to divide the cronjobs into groups/sets, and run them separately.

In the coming chapters, we'll set up some cronjobs: clear draft, start workflow event, and notification.

Configuration files

The default configuration files end with a .ini extension and are located in the settings directory. Each file controls the behavior of a specific part of the system. The main and the most important configuration file is called site.ini. Among other things, this file tells eZ Publish which database, design, and so on, should be used. The default configuration files contain all of the possible directives (with default settings), along with brief explanations. These files should only be used for reference, and should never be modified.

An eZ Publish configuration file is divided into blocks. Each block contains a collection of settings. For example:

```
...
# This line contains a comment.
[DatabaseSettings]
Server=localhost
User=allman
Password=qwerty
Socket=disabled
SQLOutput=enabled

# This line contains another comment.
[ExtensionSettings]
ActiveExtensions[]=ezdhtml
ActiveExtensions[]=ezpaypal
...
```

The example above shows two blocks: DatabaseSettings and ExtensionSettings. Each block has several sub-settings, which control the behavior of the system. A setting can usually be set to enabled/disabled, a string of text, or an array of strings. If the name of the setting ends with a pair of square brackets, it means that the setting accepts an array of values. In the example above, the ActiveExtensions setting tells eZ Publish to use two different extensions: ezdhtml and ezpaypal. Lines starting with a hash mark (#) are treated as comments.

As pointed out earlier, the default configuration files should never be modified because they will most likely be overwritten by a new set of files during an upgrade. Because of this, custom configuration settings must be placed elsewhere. Global configuration overrides can be placed in the /settings/override directory. The settings of the configuration files located in this directory will override the default settings. The name of the configuration files in the override directory must end with extension .ini.append.php or .php.

If an override configuration file exists with both extensions, eZ Publish will process the one with the .ini.append.php extension. The .php extension is more secure, because will be processed by the web server as a PHP script. If someone attempts to read it directly using browser software, the server will not display the contents because the configuration settings are commented out. This method will prevent the disclosure of secure information such as the database username and password.

In order for this to work, the contents of the configuration file must be encapsulated by a pair of PHP comment markers: /* and */. The following example shows how an override (for example test.ini.append.php) should be set up:

```
<?php /*
#?ini charset="utf-8"?
# These are my example settings
[ExampleSettings]
ExampleSettingOne=enabled
ExampleSettingTwo=disabled
...

*/ ?>
```

The charset directive reveals the character set that was used to construct the .ini file (usually UTF-8).

The setup wizard

We have now prepared the system and downloaded the required software but we have not yet used the software. We have to do the last step in order to start creating our magazine site.

Let's open a browser and enter the URL http://packtmediaproject. The setup wizard, provided by eZ Publish will start to configure our new site. Following the setup wizard is quite easy and we'll take a look at all of the pages that we have to visit before using the CMS.

Welcome to eZ Publish

The first page we will see is the welcome page for eZ Publish. Here we can see the welcome message for the installation, and we can click on **Next** to proceed to the actual installation.

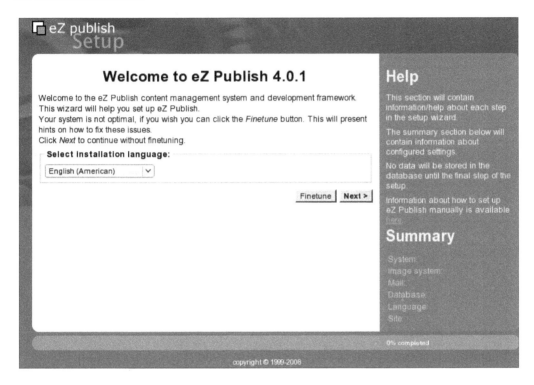

System check

If you forget some aspect of configuration or your system needs some more fixes, the system check page lists all the detected issues. Follow the instructions, one-by-one, to fix the problems. Every time you click on the **Next** button, the wizard will run the System Check again, and if no more issues are found you can continue. Sometimes it is necessary to ignore a configuration; in this case you need to select the **Ignore this test** checkbox as seen in the next screenshot:

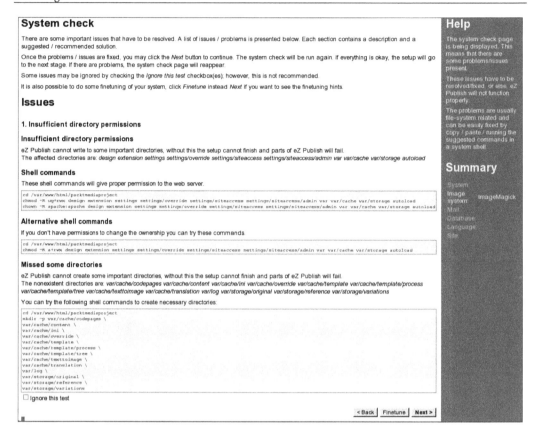

The **Finetune** button is used for tuning the whole system to work best with the CMS. This procedure is optional and it should only be used if you have a highly-customized PHP configuration.

Email settings

After the system has been configured, we need to set up our outgoing email settings. We assume you shall want to use the sendmail SMTP server, which is usually installed on all main Linux distributions.

If your server is configured to not use sendmail (or some compatible MTAs such as Postfix or Qmail) you'll have to use SMTP configuration. In this case, you have to specify the SMTP server name (or its IP address) and the user and password (if needed) to send outgoing emails.

Choose a database

After we finish configuring all of the email stuff, we have to move on to the database side.

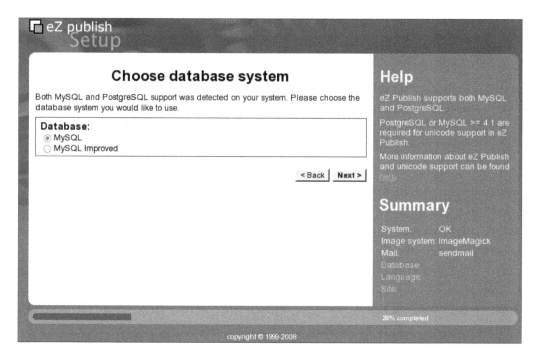

In this step we can choose our database engine. eZ Publish supports MySQL, MySQLi and PostgreSQL. In the list are present only the engines configured with our PHP installation.

If you have configured only MySQL as the PHP database, this page will not be shown.

If the PHP is configured to use **mysqli extensions**, then the setup wizard will suggest that you use this. This choice is recommended, as it guarantees good performance.

Database initialization

After we have chosen our DBMS, we need to provide the necessary information for the system to connect to the database.

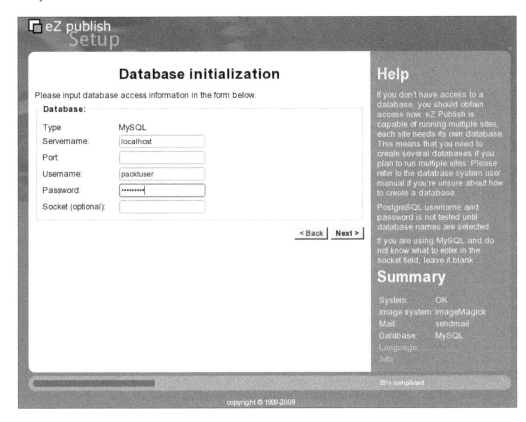

To set up our site we have to use **localhost** as the server name, **packname** as username, and **packtpwd** (or an alternative password, if you prefer) for the password.

When the **Next** button is clicked, the wizard will try to connect to the database. If it fails, then the database initialization page will be shown again.

Language support

The language support page allows you to choose the primary language for the eZ Publish installation.

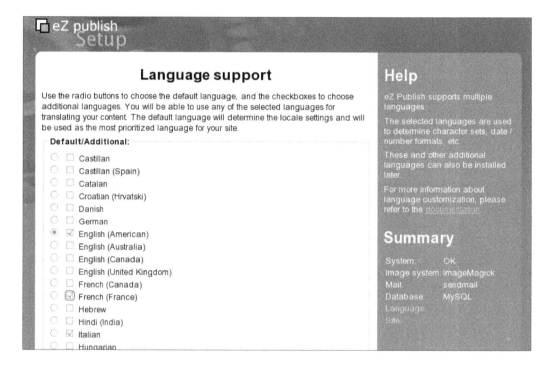

We can also choose other additional languages (in our example we have chosen Italian, French, and English) that will be used to translate content.

The system allows us to reconfigure and add languages at any time, so if you add more languages you can change these settings after the complete installation. It is very important to note that choosing a primary language will also set up the localization of the CMF. So, for example, the type of default date format will change from US format to an Italian one.

Site packages

As we said before, eZ Publish has some site packages bundled by default. In this section of the wizard, we can select the main package that we will use to develop our site.

All of the packages can be installed and used together, but we don't suggest that you do this. Instead, focus on a single package, and if really necessary extend this through the use of components and extensions.

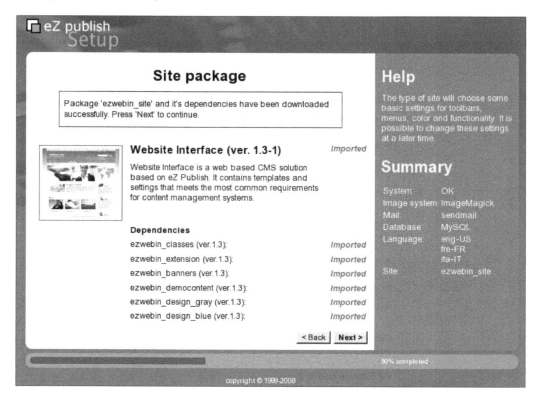

For our Magazine site we will use the **eZ Webin** extension, which is bundled in the **Website Interface packages**.

 It is important to allow the server to download content from the Internet. This will be necessary should you want to download all of the packages needed by the **eZ Webin** extension. If your server is behind a firewall then you will have to create a file called site.ini.append.php in the setting/override directory, and add the following lines to it:

```
[ProxySettings]
ProxyServer=proxy.domain.com:8080
User=proxyUser
Password=proxyPassword
```

Replace proxy.domain.com:8080 with the actual proxy address, and restart the Setup Wizard.

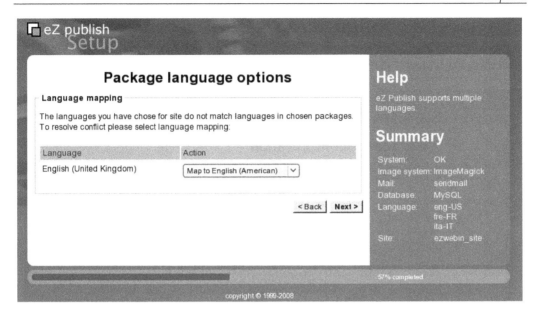

When we select a non-English default language, it is possible that the site package that we install will have no support. In this case, the setup wizard allows three kinds of actions:

1. Map the package language to one of our choices, so that the missing text will be replaced with the default one.
2. Create a new language.
3. Don't create the content for the language.

In our case, we decide to map all of the existing English (UK) content to English (American). Then (if needed) we can update this, according to our needs, later on.

Site access configuration

In this step, we can select the access method we want to use in eZ Publish. This is a very important step and the usage of the CMS strictly inherits from this choice.

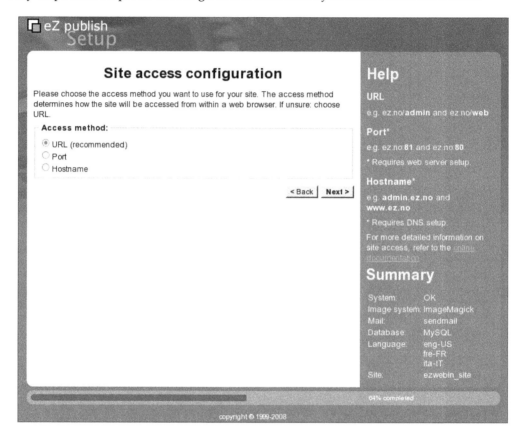

The system allows three possible choices:

- **URL (recommended)**: This is the default, and recommended, value. It doesn't require any particular configuration. It simply uses an HTTP request to the main index.php file to facilitate site access.

- **Port**: The Port configuration is used to map a site to a particular port on our server, for example http://packmediaproject:81/. To use this parameter, it is necessary to change the Apache configuration and handle all of the possible conflicts with proxies and the firewall.

- **Hostname**: This last option is used, for example, to map the site to a unique hostname (for example, a subdomain on the backend). As with the Port option, it a web server and a DNS configuration is necessary.

Site details

On this page, the wizard will show all of the set-up information. Moreover it shows the databases installed on our system.

Now, we have to select the `packmediaproject` database, which we have previously created. Do this by selecting it from the drop-down box and clicking on the **Refresh** button.

If the database is not empty, the wizard will ask what you want to do:

- Keep the existing data and add the new tables
- Choose another database
- Remove the existing data
- Leave the data as it is (do not add the new tables)

Site security

This is the last actual configuration step. Here, we will add base security to our system to prevent it from being used by unknown users.

To do this, we only need to fill the form with the data that will be used by the administrator. It's very important to specify a *real email* address so that it is possible to change the password if forgotten.

Site registration

Site registration is an optional step that allows eZ System to know if sites using eZ Publish are online or not.

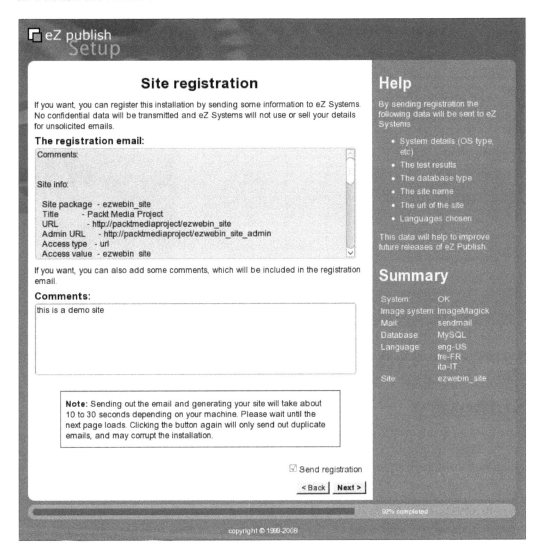

All of the sent data will be confidential, and used by eZ System's staff to check the different types of platforms used for eZ Publish. Feel free to send or not send the notification.

Finished

Now our site is online and we can start working on it.

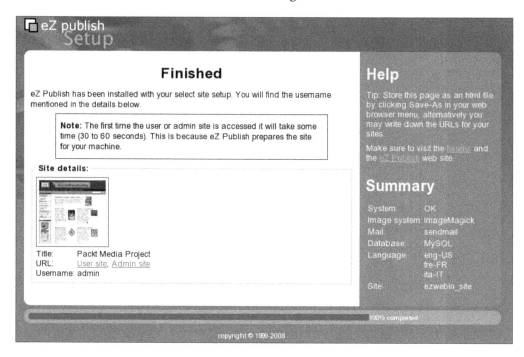

Don't forget to bookmark both the **User site** and the **Admin site** links.

Summary

Now we know what eZ Publish is, and what we mean by the CMF initialism. We have learned about the components that eZ Publish uses to operate, and how to install and configure them.

In this chapter, we have also seen how to install the whole eZ Publish CMS through the Setup Wizard tool, and how to choose the best site package to fulfill our needs. In the next chapter, we will work on the eZ Publish site access, to have a multilingual, enabled site.

2
Creating Our Siteaccesses

An eZ publish installation can host multiple sites using something called the siteaccess system

— *eZ.no site*

In this chapter we will look at:

- eZ Publish siteaccesses
- How to create custom siteaccesses
- How a custom site access will help us in development stage

Also, we will look at how to enable additional languages on our site.

What is the siteaccess system?

To override eZ Publish's default configuration, we need to create a collection of configuration settings called siteaccess. The role of a siteaccess is to indicate to eZ which database, design, and `var` directory should be used for a particular context.

With siteaccess it is possible to use the same content and different designs (for example, when creating a mobile version of our site) or do the opposite (for example, managing a multilingual site where the template doesn't change but the content does).

It's also possible to create an administration siteaccess, where we can manage any kind of content, such as users, media files and, of course, the articles, or a frontend siteaccess that is the website, where we can only view the public published content.

A typical eZ publish site consists of two siteaccesses: a public interface for visitors and a restricted interface for editors. In this case, both siteaccesses use the same content, but different designs. Whereas the administration siteaccess would most likely use the built-in administration design, the public siteaccess would probably use a custom design.

The following illustration, taken from the official eZ Publish documentation, shows this scenario:

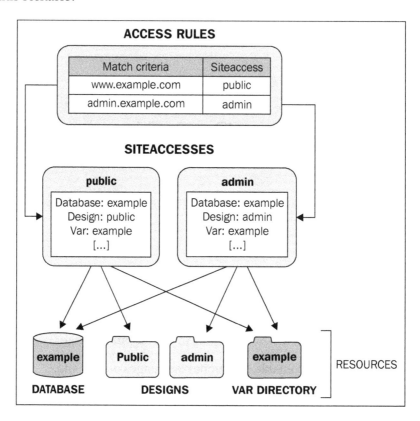

Usually, in big projects it is also useful to have two additional siteaccesses: a *staging siteaccess* and a *developing siteaccess*. The first is used in a staging environment to make frequent deployments of modifications that can be tested by the customer (in this case, the siteaccess uses a different database but the same design as for the public and admin siteaccesses). The second one, instead, is used by developers on their local machine (this siteaccess uses a local database, but once again uses the same design as for the public and admin siteaccesses).

A single eZ publish installation can host a virtually unlimited number of sites by simply adding new siteaccesses, designs, and databases.

Siteaccess folder structure

The configuration settings for siteaccesses are located inside a dedicated subfolder within the `/settings/siteaccess` folder. The name of the subfolder is the actual name of the siteaccess.

It is very important to remember that a siteaccess name can only contain letters, numbers, and underscores.

The following illustration shows a setup with two siteaccesses: admin and public.

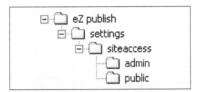

When a siteaccess is in use, eZ publish reads the configuration file in the following sequence:

- Default configuration settings: `/settings/*.ini`
- Siteaccess settings: `/settings/siteaccess/[name_of_siteaccess]/*.ini.append.php`
- Global overrides: `/settings/override/*.ini.append.php`

eZ Publish will first read the default configuration settings. Then, it will determine which siteaccess to use based on the rules that are defined in the global override for `site.ini` `/settings/override/site.ini.append.php`. When it knows which siteaccess has to be used, it will go into the correct siteaccess folder and read the configuration files that belong to that siteaccess. The settings of the siteaccess will override the default configuration settings.

For example, if a siteaccess uses a database called `packtmediaproject_test`, the system will find this and automatically use the specified database when an incoming request is processed.

Finally, eZ Publish reads the configuration files in the global override directory. The settings in the global override directory will override all other settings. So, if a database called `packtmediaproject` is specified in the global override directory for `site.ini`, then eZ publish will attempt to use that database regardless of what is specified in the siteaccess settings.

If a setting is not overridden either by the siteaccess, or from within a global override, then the default setting will be used. The default settings are set by the .ini files located in the /settings directory. The following figure illustrates how the system reads the configuration files, using the site.ini file as an example:

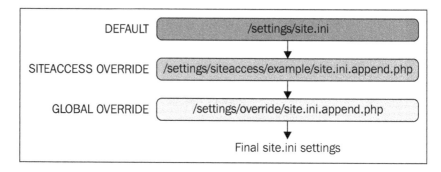

Creating a siteaccess for dev, staging, and production environments

Once we have finished installing eZ Publish, we'll find a folder called setting/siteaccess, with the default siteaccess automatically configured.

In our case we'll find these folders:

- admin: This folder usually isn't used as siteaccess, but it contains a standard configuration file that can be used to set up the administration panel

- setup: This folder contains all of the configuration files that are used during the installation process

- ezwebin_site: This is where the main design is imported directly from the eZ.no site for the package eZ Webin

- ita, eng, fre: Last but not least, the ita, eng, and fre folders have the configuration files used by the site to enable internationalization and localization

The ezwebin_site_admin is created by the webmin site package, and contains all of the configuration files for the administration panel.

Enterprise siteaccess schema

In an enterprise development process, it is very important to have four more siteaccesses:

- `dev`
- `dev_panel`
- `staging`
- `staging_panel`

The siteaccesses `dev` and `dev_panel` will be used as a development playground installation, which can be used by the development team members, with their own configuration parameters, such as database connection, path, and debug file. This will help them to test different configuration parameters or extensions without impacting the production site.

The siteaccesses `staging` and `staging_panel` will be used as a staging arena that can be used by a customer to evaluate new functionality before it is released to production. Usually, the staging installation is installed on a clone of the production server, to make sure that everything works in the same way. In our case, and for this book, we will work on the same server to better understand how to create the different siteaccesses.

All siteacccesses will have some configuration files in common, and sometimes these have to assign the same value to the parameters specified inside them. For example, if you need to create a new language siteacccess, you'll need to copy the same module configuration files to be sure that they will work in the same way for all of the languages. In this case, it will be useful to create a symbolic link from one siteaccess to another. If you don't know what a Linux symbolic link is, you can think of it as a virtual pointer to a real file, like a Windows XP shortcut.

Creating siteaccesses for dev and staging

In our case, in the `dev` and `staging` siteaccesses, we will create the following symbolic links from the `eng` folder siteaccess:

- `browse.ini.append.php`
- `contentstructuremenu.ini.append.php`
- `design.ini.append.php`
- `image.ini.append.php`
- `menu.ini.append.php`
- `odf.ini.append.php`
- `template.ini.append.php`
- `toolbar.ini.append.php`

Open a shell, and in the eZ Publish installation folder, use the `ln` (link) command to create the new symbolic links from the existing siteaccess configuration file:

```
# cd setting/siteaccess
# ln -s eng/browse.ini.append.php  dev/browser.ini.append.php
# ln -s eng/contentstructuremenu.ini.append.php dev/contentstructuremenu.ini.append.php
# …
# ln -s eng/toolbar.ini.append.php dev/toolbar.ini.append.php
```

It is very important to execute the `ln` command for all of the files listed above, to ensure that the siteaccess will not inherit the settings from the default configuration files.

Creating symbolic links

Next, we have to create more symbolic links for the configuration files in the `staging_panel` and `dev_panel` folder. So we'll create them from the `ezwebin_site_admin` files.

This is the file list:

- `contentstructuremenu.ini.append.php`
- `icon.ini.append.php`
- `odf.ini.append.php`
- `override.ini.append.php`
- `toolbar.ini.append.php`
- `viewcache.ini.append.php`

Use the same command as before, this time specifying the starting folder (`ezwebin_site_admin`):

```
# ln -s ezwebin_site_admin/browse.ini.append.php  dev_panel/browser.ini.append.php
```

We need to repeat this command for each file listed before.

Next, we will have to copy the following files from the `eng` folder to `dev` and `staging`. We have to copy these files because we will change them according to our needs in the next chapter.

- `content.ini.append.php`
- `override.ini.append.php`
- `site.ini.append.php`

We also need to copy the following files from the `ezwebin_site_admin` folder to `dev_panel` and `staging_panel`:

- `content.ini.append.php`
- `site.ini.append.php`

Configuring the database parameters

The last step is to configure the parameters related to the database connection for the staging and development installations, modifying all of the files named `site.ini.append.php` found inside the different siteaccess folders.

Open a shell and go to the eZ Publish installation folder. Then go into the `settings/siteaccess` folder and for each siteaccess that you have created, you need to edit the file `site.ini.append.php`, adding the following code, if it is not already present, at the top of the file:

```
[DatabaseSettings]
DatabaseImplementation=ezmysql
Server=localhost
Port=
User=root
Password=
Database=packtmediaproject
Charset=
Socket=disabled
SQLOutput=disabled
```

As we create the siteaccesses, we have to add them to the `site.ini.append.php` file in the `settings/override` folder . Copy the following code into the file:

```
[SiteSettings]
..
SiteList[]=dev
SiteList[]=dev_panel
SiteList[]=staging
SiteList[]=staging_panel
..

[SiteAccessSettings]
..
AvailableSiteAccessList[]=dev
AvailableSiteAccessList[]=dev_panel
AvailableSiteAccessList[]=staging
AvailableSiteAccessList[]=staging_panel
..
```

```
RelatedSiteAccessList[]=dev
RelatedSiteAccessList[]=dev_panel
RelatedSiteAccessList[]=staging
RelatedSiteAccessList[]=staging_panel
```

Creating multilingual siteaccesses

As we saw, eZ Publish created a siteaccess for every language that we enabled in the first chapter. If we'd like to add more languages for our site, we need to create a new siteaccess folder and configure the language settings inside it.

Let's create, for example, a German siteaccess. This task can be summarized in the following three steps:

1. Create a new folder called `de`, inside `settings/siteaccess/`.
2. Copy the files or create the appropriate symbolic links as per the `eng` siteaccess, inside the `de` folder.
3. Configure the siteaccess `.ini` configuration files for the language.

Copying the configuration file

We need to create all of the `.ini` files from the main language siteaccess in the new language folder (`de`). To do this, we need to create a symbolic link for all the files, except the `site.ini.append.php`, that are to be copied into the new folder.

Editing ini files for locale components

Configure all of the `site.ini.append.php` files for all of the languages siteaccesses, to enable the new German language.

To do this we will edit the files, adding the highlighted code:

```
# vi settings/siteaccess/eng/site.ini.append.php

[RegionalSettings]
Locale=eng-GB
ContentObjectLocale=eng-GB
ShowUntranslatedObjects=enabled
SiteLanguageList[]=eng-GB
SiteLanguageList[]=ita-IT
SiteLanguageList[]=fre-FR
SiteLanguageList[]=de-DE
TextTranslation=disabled
```

Do the same for the `site.ini.append.php` files in the `fre` folder and the `ita` folder.

After that, we need to copy the `eng/site.ini.append.php` to our new folder, `de`, and edit it as follows:

```
[RegionalSettings]
Locale=de-DE
ContentObjectLocale=de-DE
ShowUntranslatedObjects=enabled
SiteLanguageList[]=de-DE
SiteLanguageList[]=eng-GB
SiteLanguageList[]=ita-IT
SiteLanguageList[]=fre-FR
TextTranslation=enabled
```

The directive `SiteLanguageList` tells us the order in which the system will show the content for our objects. If the content isn't translated into German, eZ will show the English version; if the English version is unavailable than it will show the Italian one, and so on.

The last step is to add the new languages inside the `settings/override/site.ini.append.php`, as we did for the `dev` and `staging` siteaccesses:

```
[SiteSettings]
..
SiteList[]=fre
SiteList[]=ita
SiteList[]=eng
SiteList[]=de

[SiteAccessSettings]
..
AvailableSiteAccessList[]=fre
AvailableSiteAccessList[]=eng
AvailableSiteAccessList[]=ita
AvailableSiteAccessList[]=de
..
RelatedSiteAccessList[]=fre
RelatedSiteAccessList[]=eng
RelatedSiteAccessList[]=ita
RelatedSiteAccessList[]=de
```

Selecting a siteaccess using host or URI-based matching

As we saw in the first chapter, eZ publish can work using host or URI-based access.

Using the wizard, we selected the URI access method. This can be changed, if necessary, in the global override for the `site.ini` configuration file: `/settings/override/site.ini.append.php`. The behavior of the siteaccess system is controlled by the `MatchOrder` setting within the [SiteAccessSettings] block.

URI

This is the default setting for the `MatchOrder` directive, and is set by the setup wizard. When this access method is used, the name of the siteaccess that we want to use has to be the first parameter that appears after the `index.php` part of the requested URL.

For example, the following URL will tell eZ publish to use the `panel` siteaccess: `http://packmediaproject/index.php/panel`. If we want to use the `ita` siteaccess, then the URL that we have to call will be `http://packmediaproject/index.php/ita`. If nothing is used in the last part of the URL, then the default siteaccess will be used.

Setting the default siteaccess

The default siteaccess is defined by the `DefaultAccess` setting within the [SiteSettings] section. To change it, we have to open the `/settings/override/site.ini.append.php` file and make the changes highlighted here:

```
[SiteSettings]
DefaultAccess=ita
[SiteAccessSettings]
MatchOrder=uri
```

The URI access method is very useful for the development/preview stage where changing the DNS server isn't very easy.

Host

The host access method makes it possible to map different host/domain combinations to different siteaccesses. This access method requires the configuration of the server and DNS (not eZ Publish). The DNS server must be configured to resolve the desired host/domain combinations to the IP address of the web server, and then the web server must be configured to trigger a virtual host configuration (unless eZ Publish is located in the main document root). Once these settings are configured properly, eZ Publish can be set up to use different siteaccesses based on the host/domain combinations of the incoming requests.

The following example shows how to set up /settings/override/site.ini. append.php in order to make eZ Publish use the host access method. In addition, it reveals the basic usage of the host matching mechanism.

```
[SiteAccessSettings]
MatchOrder=host
HostMatchType=map
HostMatchMapItems[]=www.packmediaproject.com;eng
HostMatchMapItems[]=it.packmediaproject.com;ita
```

The example above tells eZ publish to use the eng siteaccess, if the requested URL starts with www.packmediaproject.com. If the requested URL starts with it.packmediaproject.com, the Italian version of the site will be used.

In the same way, we can configure HostMatchMapItems to use the admin panel and other languages. Using the host configuration is useful if we don't want to make the backend subdomain public, but want to make it internal to our network, or to support those sites that want to differentiate the languages instances with a dedicated subdomain.

Summary

In this chapter we learned what a siteaccess is, and how to configure and personalize it. We also learned how to add more languages to our sites, and how to change the access method from URL to Host mode.

In the next chapter, we will meet the eZ Publish content classes, and will define the main content classes for our project.

3
Defining and Creating Content Classes

To make a table we need some wood
to make some wood we need a tree
to make a tree we need a seed ...

"Ci vuole un fiore", a children's song by Gianni Rodari

In this chapter, we will look at what the content class is for eZ Publish, and how to create and manage it. We will define all of the content classes needed by our site to create articles and staff profile pages.

Before opening a browser and starting to create new content classes, we have to take a few minutes to learn what a content class is, how eZ Publish manages the content, and how this content will help us in our work. We also need to decide what we will want to publish on the site by defining all of the appropriate content classes.

Managing the content

One of the main scopes of a CMS is to manage any kind of content and data structure with as little effort for the users as possible. So it is very important to handle the content with enough flexibility to allow choosing what to show and what not to show in any possible context.

For example, a good CMS should allow us to store a lot of information on an article, useful for internal use, and choose not to show on the site frontend, because it is not necessary for readers. Or, instead, a CMS, gives us the ability to update our articles by adding information and rewriting them easily.

So, we not only need a complete decoupling of the content from the design, but also the ability to manage the content in different possible ways.

Separation of content and design

If the content can be defined as the action to store data in some way, the purpose of the design is to display that data. One of the key features of eZ Publish is the complete separation of content and design. This gives the ability to create different kinds of content structure and reuse them for different purposes, permitting developers and designers to work separately, publish content in different formats, and rewrite a complete interface without any development issue.

Content structure in eZ Publish

Unlike other CMS platforms, eZ Publish doesn't assign a fixed content type based on a strict definition.

However, it uses the content class paradigm. Any kind of content is a content class that is built on top of a content attribute. A user can, at any time, merge in different attributes to create a new content class, or edit an existing one. Moreover, a developer can also create a new content attribute to extend the system without any virtual limits.

Object-oriented content

As we say, all of the content classes are defined by one or more attributes, and each of these attributes are defined by an input field. So, we can say that eZ Publish uses an object-oriented approach to describe the content, where the main object inherits the attributes' characteristics and exposes them to the user as input forms.

Moreover, we have to understand that when we talk about content classes, we are not talking about its data. The content classes are only the definitions of the content object structure. Content objects, however, are instances of content classes in which we can store our data.

For example, we can use the following image from the eZ Publish documentation, where we have the **Article** content class that is used to generate three different **Article objects**:

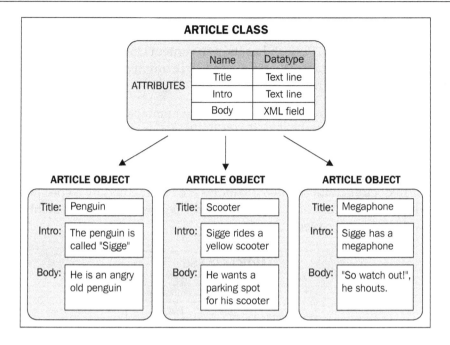

As we can see in the next image from the official eZ System documentation, a content object should have one or more versions. Now, this version should be both a *translation* and a *revision* of the object itself, and should be able to be placed as a **node** inside the *content tree* of eZ Publish.

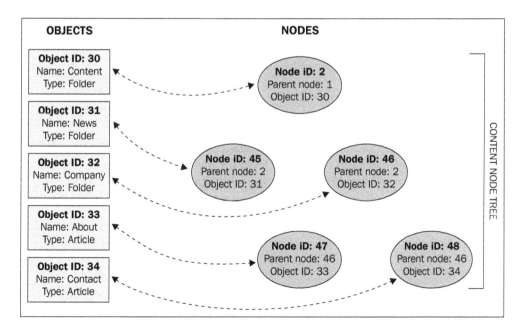

eZ Publish content classes

Every type of content in eZ Publish has its own content class, but we have to clearly understand that a content class doesn't store any type of data; it represents a definition of a data structure.

For example, if our site shows some stories on the home page, these stories should be defined by an *Article* content class that is built on one or more attributes, such as Title, Body, and Publication date.

These attributes are called *Class Attributes*. As we can see in the following image from the eZ Publish documentation, these attributes are represented by a specific datatype (which is the smallest entity of storage) and describe how a specific content has to be retrieved, validated, and saved:

ARTICLE CLASS

	Name	Datatype
ATTRIBUTES	Title	Text line
	Intro	Text line
	Body	XML field

Class attributes

The class attributes are defined by four elements:

- The name
- The generic control
- The internal identifier
- The datatype-specific controls

The name is the *friend name* used to store the class attribute and it will be used, for example, in the administration panel as a label for the input form. The name can contain letters, digits, special characters (also whitespaces), and can be up to 255 characters long. If it is left empty, eZ will assign a unique value. A valid name value could be: `The lastname of the author`:

Whereas the name is designed for users, the internal identifier is needed by the system to simply identify an attribute during the programming task. In this case, the string must be no more than 50 characters long and should not contain any special characters. Also, the space character is banned and underscores must be used instead. A valid internal identifier value could be: author_lastname.

Any datatype has four generic controls available by default. They are **Required**, **Searchable**, **Translatable**, and **Information Collector**. As the first three are self-explanatory, we have to spend some words only for the last control.

The Information Collector control enables eZ Publish to store input directly from the site's frontend. When a class attribute has this flag enabled, it will always act as an input form and will store all of the data inserted into it. We should take as an example a comment form where a user should leave his name, email, and (of course) a text comment. These three inputs are generated by three class attributes with the information collector control flagged as true.

Whereas the generic controls are assigned to all kinds of class attributes, the specific controls are defined in the datatype structure. For example, if we use the class attribute built on the Date datatype, then we will be provided with the *Default value* control. But if we choose the Image datatype (a datatype specialized in managing image files) instead, an additional specific control, *Max file size value*, will be added.

Datatypes

eZ Publish, by default, exposes a lot of different types of datatypes. A datatype is the smallest entity of storage, and can be mixed to create complex content classes. A custom datatype must be created directly in PHP. It can't be generated by the web interface. To see which datatypes are enabled in the 4.0.x release of eZ Publish, we suggest reading the reference book published on the ez.no site at http://ez.no/doc/ ez_publish/technical_manual/4_0/reference/datatypes.

Content class management

Now let's understand how eZ Publish gives us the ability to manage the content classes from the administration panel. Open a browser and go to the domain URL we configured in the installation chapter, specifying the administration panel path we chose in Chapter 2. If you previously didn't change anything, you should open the administration panel directly from `http://packtmediaproject/ezwebin_site_admin url`. Here, you can log in using "admin" as username and the password that you chose in the setup wizard.

Now, click on the **Setup** label in the main navigation bar and then select **Classes** in the left sidebar.

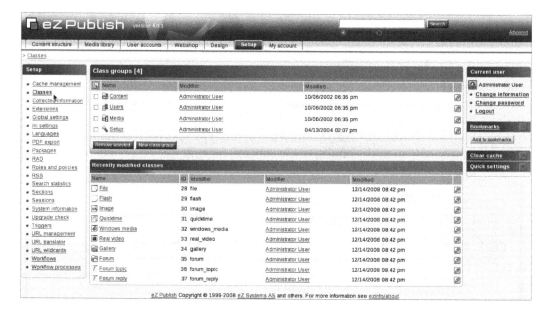

You will see the main classes page where all of the default eZ Publish content classes created for the eZ Webin package are defined. The central column of the page is divided into two main rows. The first row defines the default **Class groups** (where the default classes are stored) and the second row shows you the latest changes made by a user.

If we click on the group labeled **Content**, we will see all of the default classes that we should use to create our site.

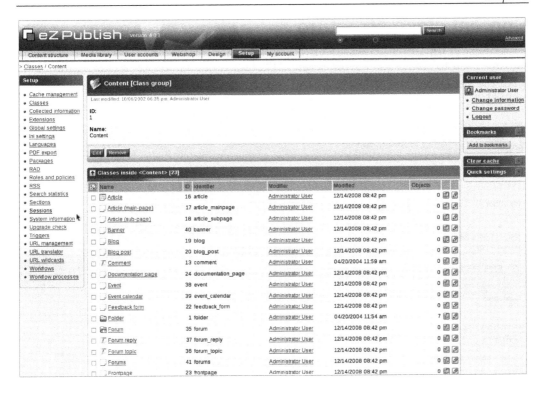

Default content classes reference

When we install eZ Publish with the eZ Webin package, we also install
a lot of preconfigured content classes that can be used "out of the box"
(for example: article, blog post, forum, comment, and so on.). Moreover,
all of the site packages, plugins, or extensions should add more content
classes to fulfill their tasks. You will see the main content class defined
in the eZ.no reference site at `http://ez.no/doc/ez_publish/`
`technical_manual/4_0/reference/content_classes`.

Now click on the **Edit** link for the `Article` class to take a look at the classes attributes
and structure.

Content class structure

As we saw in the previous sections, eZ Publish installs some default content classes that are used to create a site from scratch. For example, the `Article` class contains all of the structures needed to store and publish news articles as a title, body, and so forth.

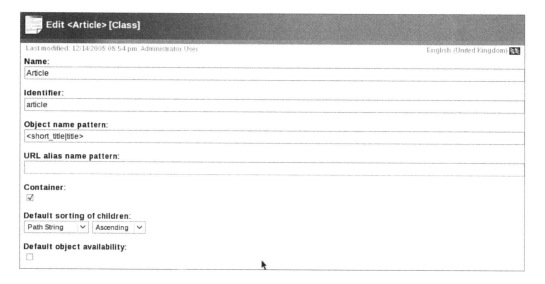

The structure of a class is divided into class properties and class attributes. The `Article` class properties are:

Name	Identifier	Container	Object name pattern	URL alias name pattern	Default sorting of children	Default object availability
Article	article	yes	`<short_title|title>`	`<short_title>`	Path String / Ascending	No

Just as we did for the class attributes, let's describe the meaning of these properties.

Name

The *Name* property is used to store a friendly name that describes the defined class. As for the class attribute's name definition, it can have up to 255 characters and can contain letters, digits, and special characters. If nothing is defined, then eZ Publish will create a unique name.

Identifier

The identifier of a content class works exactly like the attributes. It can accept only digits, letters, and underscores and cannot be longer than 50 characters.

Object name pattern

This property is used to automatically name all instances of a class. For example, if we create an article titled *packmediasite is the best book*, the system will translate it into a valid object name. All of the text inside the angular brackets has to be an attribute identifier, whereas the text outside it will be added as-is.

URL alias name pattern

This property works exactly like the Object name pattern, and is used to define the URL aliasing for an object. If left blank, the object name will be used instead.

Container checkbox

If this checkbox is selected, then the attribute will act as a container. This means that it will be rendered as a form and all of the data inserted by a user will be stored in the eZ Publish storage area.

Default sorting of children

On setting this property, it is possible to handle the instances of this content class if they are defined as containers, order of their children (or subitem) list. For example, if we select an ascending order for the Article class children, and a descending order for the comment class, then this property gives only a default behavior for the class. But it can be personalized for all single class instances.

Attributes

We saw in the previous pages what a class attribute is and how to manage its properties. Now let's see the default values for the `Article` attributes:

Name	Identifier	Datatype	Required	Searchable	Collector	Translatable
Title	`title`	Text line	Yes	Yes	No	Yes
Short title	`short_ title`	Text line	No	Yes	No	Yes
Author	`author`	Authors	No	Yes	No	Yes
Intro	`intro`	XML Block	Yes	Yes	No	Yes
Body	`body`	XML Block	Yes	Yes	No	Yes
Enable comments	`enable_ comments`	Checkbox	No	No	No	No
Image	`image`	Object relation	No	Yes	No	No
Keywords	`keywords`	Keywords	No	Yes	No	Yes

The content classes can be modified at any time to better adapt the site's needs. So we can add, change, or delete attributes, and in this case, all of the data will be removed automatically by the system.

 Please note that removing an attribute from a class with many instances of a content object can be dangerous. This is because the data structure of your content objects can become corrupt if the removing action finishes before it has removed all of the attributes. To prevent this, you should raise the default 30 second script execution time (`max_execution_time`) in the `php.ini` to a minimum of two or three minutes.

Packt Media Site's content class

We learned what content classes are, and now we have to create our own classes by customizing the existing ones, or creating new ones from scratch.

But first, we need to understand what we need in our site.

We will describe the Packt Media Site as the site of a youth magazine that decided to move onto the Web after some years of success in the paper market.

The magazine will publish all of the articles based on a precise editorial program. Moreover, the readers will have the possibility to comment on them in a dedicated forum.

The last point we have to fulfill is that all of the members of the editorial staff want a personal profile page where they can show their own articles and some personal data. With this information, and taking a look at the default content classes that eZ Publish gives us, the only thing we have to do is creating a personal profile page from scratch.

Creating the profile content class

We have to open the browser again and log in to the administration panel. Here, we go to the setup page, click on the **Classes** link in the sidebar, and enter the content group. On the bottom of the page, we will click on the **New class** button and start creating our new class.

The first thing we have to choose are the main properties of the content class. We will add them as shown here:

Next, we will add some attributes that will be shown on the site.

The first attribute we will use is the **Authors**. To choose it, simply select the **select** menu and then click on the **Add attribute** button. The result will be similar to the screenshot shown here:

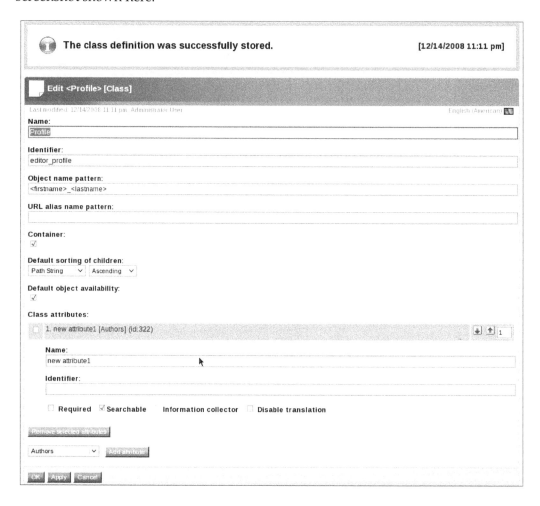

By default, eZ Publish sets a fake name (in this case, **new attribute1**) as an attribute name. We should change this to one that is easily recognizable when we work in the backend. Moreover, we should select the **Required** checkbox to be sure that a profile will always be assigned to an existing user.

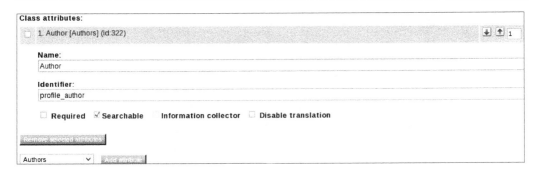

Now, we will add a new **XML block** attribute that will enable a WYSIWYG text area editor that we will use to insert the author description. As before, we will change the default values to something more expressive, like the ones shown here:

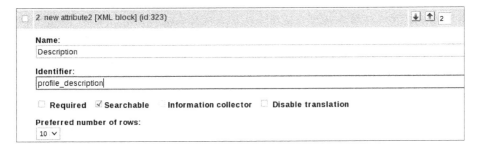

To complete our work, we need to define some more attributes such as the firstname and lastname of the editor, as well as their birth date, email, and photo.

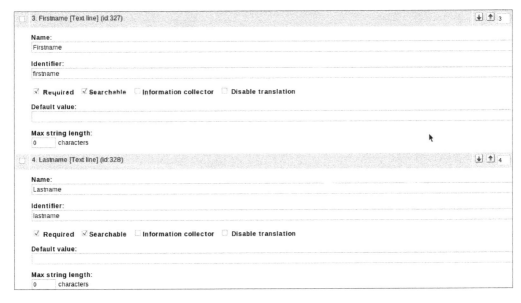

The date attribute can only store dates from 01/01/1970 to the year 2032. So, if you need to manage an older date for the birthday attribute, you need to use the Birthday Datatype extension (http://projects.ez.no/birthday). We will see how to install and manage extensions in the upcoming chapters.

The last step will be to add a **User account** attribute. Set this to "not required" (deselect the **Required** checkbox), to assign an eZ Publish user to that profile, if present.

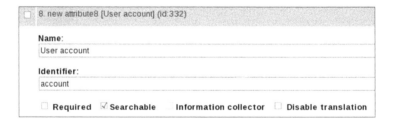

When we click on the **OK** button to confirm all of the changes that we applied to the Profile form, we are redirected to the **Profile [Class]** summary page, where we can see what we have done.

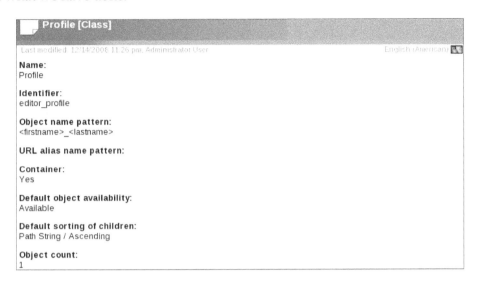

If you miss some steps, you can click on the **Edit** button and modify the created class again.

Extending the Article class

Sometimes, the articles of the magazine are written by two or more editors and we want to list all of them on the article's page. Moreover, we also want to show all of the articles written by an author.

Again, click on the **Classes** link in the sidebar. Now go to the Content folder, click on the **Article** class, and then click on the **Edit** button.

Next, add a new attribute called **Object relations**, which will enable multiple relations with other predefined objects.

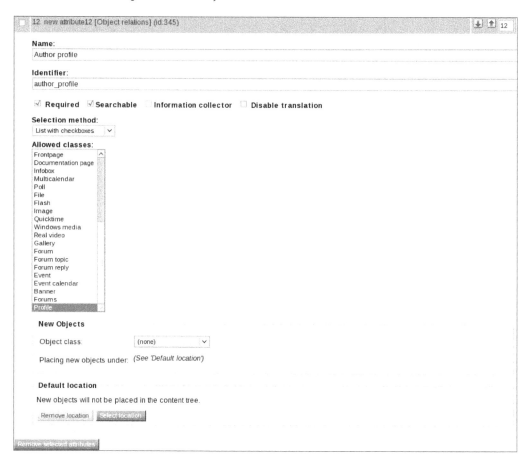

In our case, for the sake of simplicity, we will choose **List with checkboxes** as the select method. This will display a list of all the authors, preceded by a checkbox to relate one by one to the article, and we will allow only the Profile class.

Now we can save the Article class and go on to create our content classes.

The other content classes

We will now create more content classes to manage the forum and the feedback form.

But luckily, eZ Publish is very helpful and exposes some ready-to-use classes that we can use without a need to modify them in any way. These classes are the forum, the forum reply, and the feedback form classes.

Summary

In this chapter, we learned what content classes are, how to manage them, and also how eZ Publish manages the different types of content. We also started our magazine site project by creating the Profile and customizing the Article content classes.

In the next chapter we will use this work to create a content structure for the site.

4
Creating Content Structure

The Guide is definitive. Reality is frequently inaccurate.

— The Hitchhiker's Guide to the Galaxy, Douglas Adams

In Chapter 1, we installed eZ Publish; in Chapter 2, we configured the site access; and in the Chapter 3, we created the content class we have to use. Now it's time to use all of the work we did to create the new enterprise-level site for our Packt Media magazine. But before that, to better understand what we will do next, we'll introduce the eZ Publish backend and its publishing-related functionality.

In this chapter, we will:

- Learn how to use the eZ Publish backend
- Look at creating the default content structure for the magazine
- Add some initial content, so that we can use the content classes that we created in the last chapter

To begin with, let's open a browser and go to the administration panel of eZ Publish, at `http://packtmediaproject/index.php/ezwebin_site_admin`.

Understanding the backend

In Chapter 3, we focused on the **Setup** tab, and created new content classes and class attributes. Now we'll take a step back and get introduced to the backend of eZ Publish, to understand how the **Content structure** and **Media library** tabs work.

As we can see, the backend of eZ Publish is divided into four main areas:

- The navigation bar (on the top of the screen)
- The secondary menu (on the left-hand side of the screen)
- The content area
- The right-hand menu

Inside the navigation bar, we will find the main menu and a breadcrumb path.

What is a breadcrumb path?

Breadcrumbs or a *breadcrumb path* is a navigation aid used in user interfaces. It provides users with a way to keep track of their location within programs or documents. The term comes from the trail of breadcrumbs left by Hansel and Gretel in the popular fairytale.

The navigation menu contains the links to all of the main sections of the CMS, and also includes a classic breadcrumb path that helps us to understand where we are and how we get back to where we were.

The secondary menu and the content area will change, contextually, based on the CMS section we are in. The right-hand menu will only contain user- and debug-related information.

In this chapter, we won't see a description of all of the CMS section tabs in depth. We will focus only on the first two tabs. When you start using eZ Publish, you'll understand the similarities in the other sections.

Content structure

The **Content structure** section represents the site content tree that is usually seen on the frontend of the site. In the secondary menu of this section, we can see a dynamically-generated tree structure containing the content nodes, and the details of the selected node, in the content area.

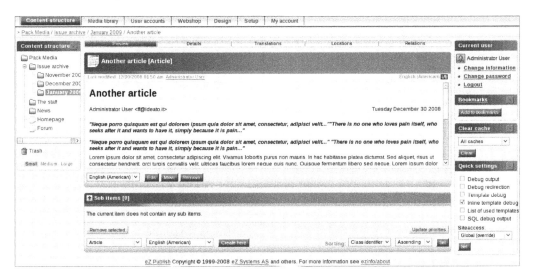

The **Media library** acts the same as the **Content structure**, but is basically a repository of all of the media content that we have uploaded into the CMS. Every time we upload something, eZ Publish will understand the type of media (audio/video, image, or other type) and will place it in the correct folder of the **Media library** section.

The secondary menu

The secondary menu is often called the left-hand menu. It contains the content tree of our site, and provides us with a shortcut to create and manage this tree.

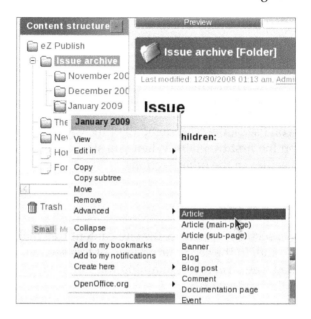

The secondary menu acts as a file browser, just as it does in some operating systems. In the content tree, you can easily see what is a folder object (that is, content containers) and what is a content object, just as you can do in Windows Explorer or Gnome Nautilus.

As with a file browser, the content tree has a context menu that is triggered when you left-click on a content icon (folder or any kind of content class). The contextual pop-up menu that appears allows you to perform many of the normal operations that can be performed via the standard interface. Moreover, it also provides access to other functionality, via the **Advanced** voice of the pop-up menu that will be enabled in particular context, such as clicking on a folder or a particular type of data.

This pop-up menu is present every time a node tree is displayed in the CMS, independent of the area. You will learn more about this when we introduce the **Sub items** box.

If you cannot display the expanded content tree, you need to configure the AJAX behavior inside the `settings/contentstructuremenu.ini` file. To do this, we will override the file and copy it into the `settings/override` directory. Then, we will open the file in a text editor, and set the `dynamic` option under the `[TreeMenu]` section to **enabled** as follows:

```
cd /var/www/packtmediaproject/settings
cp  contentstructuremenu.ini  override/
contentstructuremenu.ini.append.php

vi override/contentstructuremenu.ini.append.php

[TreeMenu]
# If set to enabled,the admin tree menu is fetched
# and built dynamically on the fly.
# Requires a web browser with AJAX support.
Dynamic=enabled
...
```

The content area

The content area is a container that is used to show the details of the active node. This information is placed in different boxes, which are either shown or hidden by the editor.

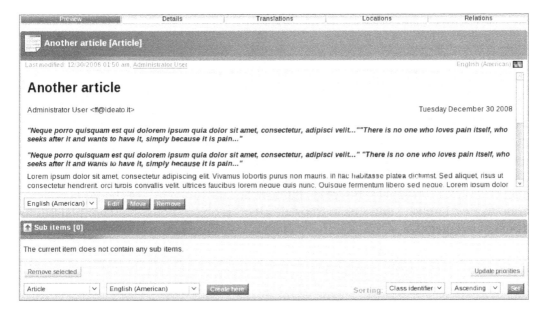

We see five tabs across the top, which, when enabled or disabled, will add information to or remove information from the content area. The tabs are:

- **Preview**
- **Details**
- **Translations**
- **Locations**
- **Relations**

Moreover, there is one more box (**Sub items**, under the box containing the object preview) that is always visible. This is related to the subitems of the object and object contextual menu. Each tab is explained in the subsections below.

Preview

This first tab is usually enabled, by default, by the CMS. It shows the content that we created, without any layout or style information. Inside this tab, the latest updated information is displayed.

Details

This tab shows information about the node history. This includes details about who created the node when, to which section it belongs, the node or object ID, and all of the counters related to the versions and translations.

Details						
Creator	Created	Section	Versions	Translations	Node ID	Object ID
Administrator User	12/30/2008 01:50 am	Standard	1	1	78	78

Translations

This tab shows what translations are available for the current node, and which translation is the default one. We can also edit or directly create a translation from this tab. We will learn how to translate our sites in Chapter 9, when we introduce the internationalization capabilities of eZ Publish. For the moment, we should bear in mind that eZ Publish allows us to translate all of its object, nodes, and templates into different languages.

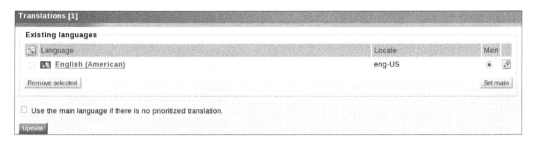

Locations

A node object of eZ Publish can be placed in several different locations. Thanks to the information tab, we can see where the current node is located and we can choose the default location. We can also set the visibility flag for single locations by enabling or disabling the content in the frontend.

Relations

This tab shows all of the relations that this object has with other objects. This tab is very useful when we have to manage content nodes that are generated by merging different objects. For example, an article that incorporates images or videos from the **Media Library**.

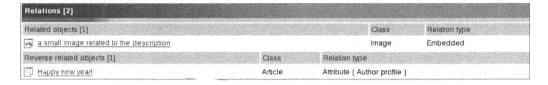

Moreover, this tab will also show the **Reverse related objects** that will help us to determine if the selected object is used elsewhere.

Sub items

Under the tabs box, there is a box called **Sub items**. This box lists all of the objects that belong to the displayed object:

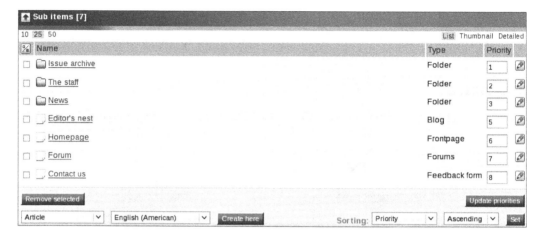

Inside this area, it is also possible to set the priority of the items. This determines the publishing order. You can also edit or create elements directly, by using the pop-up context menu, which is accessed by a click of the left button of the mouse on the node icons.

In this box, it is also possible to change the view mode by switching from the default list mode to a thumbnail mode (in which images will be displayed as thumbnails). Alternatively, you can change to a detailed view, where more information (and actions) for all of the items is displayed.

Under the **Sub item** box, there is a small select form that permits us to create new objects inside the current node.

Object contextual menu

As with the secondary menu, if we click on the icon of the selected object, a new pop-up menu will appear. This menu is strictly related to the active object, and will expose a lot of functionality, which we will use in the coming chapters.

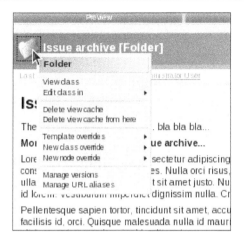

The menu gives us shortcuts to:

- See the content class of the object
- Edit the class for the enabled languages
- Delete the cache of the object, or of the related subtree
- Override the template, class, or node
- Manage the version and the URL aliases

We will go deep into the overriding and caching functionality in the coming chapters.

The content tree

As we learned in the secondary menu, which is located on the left-hand side of the **Content Structure** section, we can easily create a content tree by using a folder/object paradigm.

Now let's work on the content tree of our site.

The "Issue archive" section

We decided that we need a container for all of the past and, of course, future issues of our magazine. This container will include folders for each year (2007, 2008, 2009...), which will in turn contain subfolders based on months, into which our articles will be placed.

This simple structure will allow us to easily group the articles by issue, and use the inner functionality of the eZ Publish templating system.

To create the *Issue archive* section, we need to left-click on the site's root folder in the secondary menu, to display the context menu. We will select the **Create here | Folder** option from the context menu.

The CMS will ask us which language we want to use. Select the default language you chose in the installation chapter, and then click on the **OK** button to go to the **Edit New Folder** page.

Editing an object

When we access a content object, the main interface of eZ Publish will change slightly. Although the whole interface will appear as shown the following screenshot, we will slice it, and discuss it piece by piece:

Here, we can see on the left-hand area of the screen, all of the information relating to the content object that we are creating (or editing).

The **Object information**, especially the object **ID**, will be used to extract the data that we need in the design step. This also gives us a shortcut button to the version management page, where we can administer all of the versions of the object that we are editing.

One of the most powerful functions of the eZ Publish is the **version management** of objects.

For any object, we can create both drafts and versions. The drafts are essentially not published, but are for internal use; the versions are the published revisions of a document.

If we click on the **Manage versions** button, eZ Publish will display a new page that contains the history of the selected object. Here, we can edit or delete old versions, create new translations by copying the existing content from one version to another, and compare two different versions to see the differences between them.

This version management workflow allows the editors to coordinate the update activities better.

For example, by using the compare action, two or more editors can create different drafts for the same object version, and then merge the edited content in a new version.

Let's come back to the discussion of editing an object. In the same column, we can see the **Current draft** box, which contains information about the draft that we are working on:

The **View** button will allow us to see a preview of what we are doing inside the design template. Moreover, if we click on this button, a new section called **View control** will be displayed. This section will give us the ability to see an object in a different siteaccess context, updating the preview accordingly. It will provide a possible switchback from the preview mode, by using the **Edit** button at the bottom of the page.

The **Translate from** box allows us to create new translation, based on one of the existing ones, if there are any.

The **Section** box (shown below) is used to move content from one section of the CMS to another.

The section is usually taken from the parent node, and if we change it—for example—from **Standard** to **Media**, the object will be moved from the **Content structure** section to the **Media library** section.

At the center of the page, we can see the main editing area. This area will contain the datatypes that belong to the object that we are creating (or editing).

We'll now take a look at the Folder content class editing area, as this is a good example for the other content classes.

Every time that we create a new content object, some information will be required for some purpose. For example, for the Folder content class, the **Name** field is a required field. This name will work as a readable reference *inside* the system. But if the **Short name** is not specified, the system will use the Name to create the object URI.

In the Folder content class, we can specify values for the following fields:

- **Short Description**
- **Description**
- **Show children**
- **Tags**

Short Description and Description

These two object attributes are both XML Block datatypes. This kind of attribute integrates a WYSIWYG textarea and is usually used to manage pre-formatted content by using HTML markup.

As we can see in the following screenshot, the XML Block editor is characterized by a button bar that contains all of available tags, along with options to add or link an object, such as an image or another content node, inside the text.

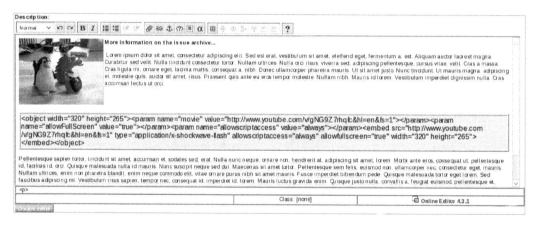

The editor is usually limited to only certain HTML tags, but can be extended by creating new custom tags. Moreover, the CMS WYSIWYG editor's philosophy is to give the authors less control on how the content should appear, in order to provide true separation between the design and the content itself. It will allow the addition of CSS classes, but will never allow a style that is not defined by the web designer.

If we click on the object button, a pop-up window will appear. This will give us two choices: upload a new object, or use an existing one.

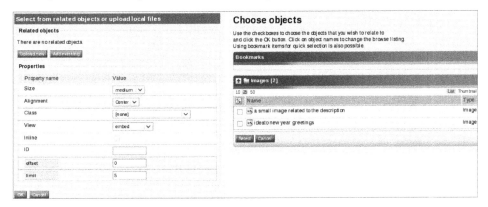

For the selected object, we can choose the attributes that we want to use, such as the size (if it is an image), the CSS style class or ID to use, and the type of view we want to apply. We can choose any content object or image, and eZ Publish will create a link or an img tag for us.

Linking objects is fundamental inside the logic of eZ Publish, because this allows the CMS to track changes to objects and to automatically update all of the content, if someone changes its position or URI.

To see the generated XML, the editor can be disabled at any time by clicking on the **Disable** editor button.

Embedding HTML inside the WYSIWYG XML Editor

There are some websites that allow us to include their widgets in our website. For example, YouTube.com allows the embedding of a video player in our site by copying some code, and SladeShare.com allows the embedding of a slides player in the same way. In eZ Publish, it's impossible to paste custom HTML codes in the XML Block attribute, but if you use the **Insert literal text** button, you can do it. All of the code added with this button will not be interpreted or checked by the eZ Publish editor, and by default, it will be rendered inside a pre tag. To override this default behavior, we have to add a new HTML class for the literal box. Then, we have to change the related configuration file and create a new template for the XML editor in our siteaccess.

To do this, open the settings/override/content.ini.append.php file with a text editor, and then add the following lines to the bottom of the file:

```
cd /var/www/packtmediaproject
vi settings/override/content.ini.append.php
...
```

```
[literal]
AvailableClasses[]=html
...
```

Now, the `html` class will appear as a choice in the literal properties, in the pop-up dialog box.

To append the code to the frontend, without using the `pre` tag, we need to create a custom template for the literal datatype in our design extension. We will learn how to do this in Chapter 6, when we talk about the template overrides.

Tags

The **Tags** input is a keyword datatype, which allows us to assign some comma-separated keywords or tags to an object.

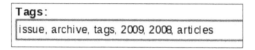

These keywords will be used to add meta information to the frontend page, and allow us to develop some other useful features, such as *related articles*.

Show children

This checkbox is present in some of the default content classes that act as containers, and is used as a trigger to show (or not) the children of the object node on the frontend of the site.

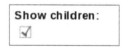

These objects will not be really hidden or made unavailable from the front page, but their link will simply disappear from inside the template of the container.

Adding more folders

After we create the first **Issue archive** folder, start over and create all of the other children folder objects.

We want to obtain a structure like the one shown in the following screenshot:

In this way, we will use the month folders to store all the related articles.

 To easily create the past year's folder, we can use the **Copy subtree** option from the context pop-up menu, by clicking on the **2008** folder icon. This action will create a complete node and subtree clone inside the node we decided to use. Now, we only need to rename the new 2008 generated note with the 2007 label.

The staff section

Now it's time to use the Profile content class that we created in Chapter 3.

As the first step, we will create a folder called **The staff**, which will contain all of the profiles of our young and cool editors. Next, we will create our first editor profile inside the folder that we just created.

We saw in the previous paragraphs how to create new objects from the secondary menu that is located in the left-hand column of the admin interface. This time, we'll use an alternative way to create our new profile objects: from the **Sub items** section.

After we select and click on **The staff** node in the left-hand menu, we will see a couple of select boxes and a **Create here** button, at the bottom of the content area.

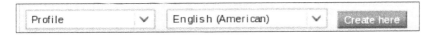

In the select box, choose the **Profile** option, and then click on the **Create here** button.

As before, the system inquires in which language we want to create the content object. Choose the default one, and continue.

The **Profile** edit page will contain all of the information that we previously added:

- A profile description
- First name and last name
- The editor's email address and birthday
- A photo upload form
- A CMS user associated to the profile (if needed)

Specify all of the necessary data, and then publish the content. Then return to the **Issue archive | 2008 | January** folder, where we will create our first article.

Creating an article

Wondering why we did not create an article content class before? The reason is in the latter part of Chapter 3. We have to add a new object relation attribute to the default article content class definition. In this way, we can relate the Profile content class to our article class. This attribute will be set as required. This means that without a published Profile object, we cannot create an article.

As we did earlier, in the select form at the bottom of the content area, choose the Article portion and then click on the **Create** button.

If the first form input of the article-editing page is very similar to those we saw in the folder, the latest attributes will introduce some new eZ Publish features. The most important ones are the time scheduling options for publishing, and the comments checkbox.

Publish and Unpublish date

These two forms will allow the eZ Publish frontend to understand if the content has to be published and/or unpublished on a certain date. All of the logic behind the time scheduling publication is handled by the design and is enabled, by default, in the package site that we downloaded during the installation of eZ Publish.

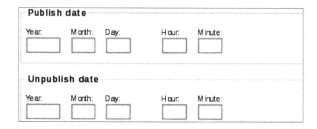

Thanks to these features, we can prepare a lot of articles in advance and then publish one of them each day, to give the readers a feeling of a truly up-to-date magazine.

This capability will also be very useful to show or hide an article teaser in the home page, or want to cycle through several content objects in a box.

Enabling comments

eZ Publish comes with a lot of preconfigured features. One such feature is the ability to enable comments to be entered for an article. This is done by selecting a checkbox in the backend, as shown here:

Every time that we select the **Enable comments** checkbox in the frontend, a **Comment** button appears under the article. When the user comments on the article, the related comment will be added as a sub-item object of the article itself.

 To enable a comment by default in our Article content class, we have to update the content class in the **Setup / Classes** section, as we saw in Chapter 2.

If a comment system is very useful for creating a good community, we will not stop here, and in the next chapters we will enable a forum system.

The feedback form

Last but not least, the final page that we have to create is the Feedback form. We will create this page directly in the root of the site by selecting the **Feedback Form** content class.

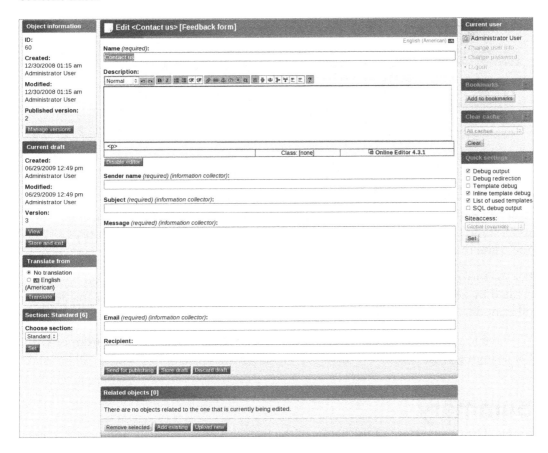

In this case, the editing form will introduce the information collector datatype that we introduced in Chapter 3.

An information collector datatype will store all of the input data directly inside the CMS, but in a different manner than the comment system. The saved data will be placed in the **Collected information** section. To access this section, you need to go to **Setup | Collected information**.

Other sections

Now we have to create more pages or sections for our site, such as the forum, some static pages such as the about page, the copyright notice or legal notices, and a site map.

For the forum, we will dedicate a whole chapter. All of the other pages can be created by adding an Article object inside the root of the content tree — or inside any other node, if you think that would be better.

We have to remember that we can create these pages at any time, in accordance with the changing requirements of the site.

Summary

In this chapter, we learned the basics of the backend of eZ Publish, and how to create and manage different types of content. We also learned how to use the context menu of the content tree.

We saw how the interface will change with the context, and understood how the content classes that we created interacted inside the system.

In the next chapter, we will create a new eZ Publish extension, in order to export our work outside of a single installation.

5
Creating an Extension

Don't repeat yourself
Pragmatic Programming

In this chapter, we will see how we can leverage the extensibility of the eZ Publish CMS to create an extension that can make our project reusable and easily portable to other installations of eZ Publish.

We will now learn how to create an extension for our project in which we'll put our new features, such as design, operators, translations, custom class definition packages, and everything else that we will build in the next chapters.

What is an extension?

In eZ Publish, an extension is like a plugin through which you can add new functionality to the CMS without changing the standard software kernel. The eZ Publish extension system is very powerful, as it allows the CMS to be extended in different ways, such as adding new features, or changing the standard behavior of the system's basic functionality.

With this system, you can keep the CMS constantly upgraded to the latest version without the fear of losing your code. In fact, in most cases, the extension will continue to run and in the worst case, you should also upgrade the extension to make it compatible with the new version.

Extension type

It's possible to create different kind of extensions, such as:

- **Operator**: This extends the standard template operators. (We will talk about them in detail in the next chapter.) For example, we can make new operator that can work with a string, or that can connect to external web services to perform some routine such as downloading content from an RSS feed.

- **Design**: This extends the standard design to customize content template with HTML and CSS, and make it easily reusable.

- **Translation**: It extends the standard XML translation files to add custom translations.

- **Workflow event**: This extends the standard workflow event, by adding a new one.

- **Module**: This extends the standard kernel modules by adding new custom modules with your own actions and views. In the custom module, it is always possible to use the powerful eZ Publish API to manage document objects and a document object tree. For example, we can make a statistic module, or a module that integrates with legacy external software with eZ Publish.

- **Fetch function:** This extends the standard fetch function by adding new functionality to implement custom queries in additional database tables.

- **Datatype**: This extends the standard datatypes with new datatypes to make the custom class more expressive.

- **Login handler**: This extends the standard authentication behaviors, by providing the ability to authenticate with external systems or legacy systems.

- **Bin**: This extends the standard shell scripts with new custom scripts.

- **Cronjob**: This extends the standard cronjob scripts with new scripts.

 In version 4.0 (of the CMS) onwards, you can also add PHP code (such as classes and interfaces) inside the extension without having to include it in the script, as this will be included automatically by the autoloading system.

The directory structure of an extension

The extension folder needs to use a standard structure to be integrated in the CMS.

In the following table, we can see the complete structure that accommodates all types of extensions:

Extension subdirectories	Description
actions/	New actions for forms
autoloads/	Definitions of new template operators or template functions
bin/	Custom shell scripts
classes/	Custom PHP classes for modules, template operators, template functions, and cronjobs
cronjobs/	Custom cronjobs scripts
datatypes/	Definitions for new datatypes
design/	Files related to the design
eventtypes/	Custom workflow events
modules/	One or more modules with views, template, and fetch functions.
packages/	Custom class packages
settings/	Configuration files
translations/	Translation files

The directory structure shown above is a complete structure, but the structure that we will use will depend on the type of extension that we need, so some directories will not be necessary. For example, a **Template Operator** extension only requires the directories autoloads/ and settings/ in a module extension. A module extension, instead, only requires the directories modules/ and settings/, and maybe the design/ directory.

For our project, we'll make an extension for extending the standard design, standard operators, standard translation files, and standard classes.

Build the extension

Now, we can create our extension called packtmedia. First, we will open our favorite file manager and then inside the eZ Publish installation folder, we will open the extension folder. In this folder, create an empty folder named packtmedia.

```
# cd /var/www/packtmediaproject
# cd extension/
# mkdir packtmedia
```

We'll use this extension to create a new design, some template operators, and our custom translations. We can now prepare the directory structure that will serve us in storing our code.

Settings extension

First, we have to create the `settings` folder that serves to override the standard configuration files (those named `*.ini.append`) and, in particular, the `site.ini.append.php` and `template.ini.append.php` files that help to enable our design, operators, and translations.

We can create this folder by executing the following commands from the installation folder of eZ Publish:

```
# cd /var/www/packtmediaproject/extension/packtmedia
# mkdir settings
# cd settings
# touch site.ini.append.php
# touch template.ini.append.php
# touch design.ini.append.php
```

Design an extension

To create a design extension, we need to create a folder named `design` in our `extension` folder, after which we will create another folder, with a custom name, inside this. This last folder will be the container for our files. We will call this folder `magazine`, and inside it we will create the following folders:

- `images`: This will contain all of the layout image files (`*.jpg`, `*.gif`, `*.png`, and so on)
- `stylesheets`: This will contain all of the stylesheet files (`*.css`)
- `javascript`: It will contain all of the JavaScript files (`*.js`)
- `templates`: This will contain all of the custom templates that will override the standard design (`*.tpl`)
- `override`: This will contain all of the override class templates (`*.tpl`)

To create these folders, we have to execute the following commands from the root folder of the eZ Publish installation:

```
# cd /var/www/packtmediaproject/extension
# cd packtmedia
# mkdir design
# cd design
# mkdir magazine
# cd magazine
```

```
# mkdir images stylesheets javascript templates override
# cd override
# mkdir templates
# cd /var/www/packtmediaproject/extension/packtmedia
```

In the end, the extension folder's structure should be created in this way:

```
packtmediaproject/extension/packtmedia/design/

                                        magazine/

                                            images/

                                            javascript/

                                            override/

                                                templates/

                                            stylesheets/

                                            templates/
```

Next, we need to add the following code to the design.ini.append.php file, which is inside the settings folder of our packtmedia extension, so that the system automatically loads our design:

```
<? /* #?ini charset="utf-8"?

[ExtensionSettings]
DesignExtensions[]=packtmedia

*/ ?>
```

> It is possible to create a custom design without an extension by just copying the packtmediaproject/extension/packtmedia/design/magazine folder into the packtmediaproject/design folder. Subsequently, it will just upload the new layout in the site.ini.append.php file of our siteaccess. The extension design is well suited to easily reusing a design in other sites, or for re-selling the layout. Not creating the extension means using an ad hoc layout for a single project, which is unlikely to be reused.

Template operator extension

To create a new extension for new template operators, we need to create the `autoloads` and the `classes` folders. In these folders, we will place the PHP classes that will be used by our scripts.

As before, to apply these changes, we will execute the following code from the root installation of eZ Publish:

 # cd /var/www/packtmediaproject/extension/packtmedia

 # mkdir autoloads

 # mkdir classes

Next, let's create the `eztemplateautoload.php` file which will be used to automatically load the template operators in the `autoloads` folder, executing the following commands:

 # cd autoloads

 # touch eztemplateautoload.php

Next, we have to write the following code inside the `eztemplateautoload.php` file:

```
<?php
$eZTemplateOperatorArray = array();
?>
```

Next, we need to add the following code to the `site.ini.append.php` file, which is inside the `settings` folder of our `packtmedia` extension, so that system automatically loads our template operators:

```
<?php /* #?ini charset="utf-8"?
...
[TemplateSettings]
ExtensionAutoloadPath[]=packtmedia
...
*/ ?>
```

We will see how to create the PHP code for a new template operator in the next chapter.

Translations extension

The next extension that we will set up will be the translation extension. This will help us manage new languages in our layout. First, we need to create the `translations` folder. Inside this folder, we can create a folder for each language that we want to translate. In our case, it will be the `fre-FR`, `ita-IT`, and `de-DE` folders because we want to translate it to Italian, German, and French.

Open a shell and then execute the following commands:

```
# cd /var/www/packtmediaproject/extension/packtmedia
# mkdir translations
# cd translations
# mkdir ita-IT
# mkdir fre-FR
# mkdir de-DE
```

 For simplicity, from now on, we will see only one of the installed languages; you can create (or edit) the others in the same way.

Next, inside the `ita-IT` folder, we have to create the `translations.ts` file executing the following commands:

```
# cd ita-IT
# touch translation.ts
```

In addition to this, we have to add the following code to the newly `translation.ts` file created before, using our preferred IDE:

```
<!DOCTYPE TS><TS>
<context>
    <name></name>
    <message>
        <source></source>
        <translation></translation>
    </message>
</context>
</TS>
```

This XML snippet is a standard placeholder for the translations that we'll see and use in the next chapters. As seen for the previous extensions, we need to add the following code to the `site.ini.append.php` file, inside the `settings` folder of the `packtmedia` extension, to make sure that the translations file is automatically loaded:

Open the file from an IDE, and then add the new `TranslationExtensions` value after the `RegionalSettings` settings, as shown:

```
<?php /* #?ini charset="utf-8"?
...
[RegionalSettings]
TranslationExtensions[]=packtmedia
...
*/ ?>
```

Activating an extension

Once we have created our extension, including the folders and the files necessary to make it work, we should activate it. Obviously, our extension is currently empty and so it does not add anything to the standard eZ Publish design. But in the next few chapters, we will complete that development with all the necessary code.

There are two ways to enable an extension. The first is to manually edit the configuration files of eZ Publish, and the second is to access the backend and enable it through a visual interface.

The first way is convenient if you want to activate the extension only for certain siteaccesses, and not in a global manner. But with the second way, you can activate the extension only for the whole installation. This means that we'll activate the extension for all of our siteaccesses.

Manual activation

To manually activate the extension for all siteaccesses, we need to change the global file `site.ini.append.php`, by executing the following commands from the shell:

```
# cd /var/www/packtmediaproject/settings/override/
# vi site.ini.append.php
```

Next, add the following code:

```
<?php /* #?ini charset="utf-8"?
...
[ExtensionSettings]
ActiveExtensions[]
...
ActiveExtensions[]=packtmedia
...
*/ ?>
```

Here, the `ActiveExtensions` parameter tells the system to enable our new extension, globally.

Or, if you want to activate the extension only for some siteaccesses, we have to modify the `site.ini.append.php` file inside every siteaccess that we want to activate it for.

To do this, we need to execute the following lines from the appropriate extension folder:

```
# cd /var/www/packtmediaproject/settings/siteaccess/ezwebin_site
# vi site.ini.append.php
```

Next, we have to add the following code:

```
<?php /* #?ini charset="utf-8"?
...
[ExtensionSettings]
ActiveAccessExtensions[]=packtmedia
...
*/ ?>
```

In this case, the `ActiveAccessExtensions` parameter will enable the extension only for the specified siteaccess.

Every time you add PHP classes that must be loaded automatically by the system autoload, you should run the script from the shell:

```
# cd /var/www/packtmediaproject
# php bin/php/ezpgenerateautoloads.php -e
```

This script will add our classes to the autoloads array.

Backend activation

Another way of enabling an extension globally is by doing so from the backend.

The following steps should be carried out to enable the extension through the graphical interface. Go to the backend of our website at `http://packtmediaproject/` `index.php/ezwebin_site_admin`, and:

1. Click on the **Setup** tab on the top menu.
2. Click on the **Extensions** link on left menu.
3. Select the **packtmedia** checkbox.
4. Click on the **Apply changes** button.

Now the extension is active.

Design activation

At this point, our extension is active, but our siteaccess will still not use our custom design. To enable the use of custom designs, we have to edit the `site.ini.append.php` file of the siteaccess. We want to use the design by executing the following commands from the shell interface:

```
# cd /var/www/packtmediaproject/settings/siteaccess/ezwebin_site
# vi site.ini.append.php
```

And now we will change the `[DesignSettings]` directive as follows:

```
<?php /* #?ini charset="utf-8"?
...
[DesignSettings]
SiteDesign=magazine
AdditionalSiteDesignList[]=ezwebin
AdditionalSiteDesignList[]=base
AdditionalSiteDesignList[]=standard
...
*/ ?>
```

In this way, our siteaccess will first use the `magazine` template designs and, if they are not present, will use the default one.

Extension portability

As from eZ Publish 3.8 version, you can install extensions through the *packages*. This system is very useful because you can install your, or third-party extensions in a very simple way through a convenient graphical interface.

From the eZ Publish backend, you can create new packages that can be used in other installations or can be freely distributed through the `ez.no` site.

To deliver our extensions and our custom classes (created in Chapter 2), we need to create two types of packages. The first one is the content classes package that will include the definition of our custom classes. The second is an extension package that will include our entire extensions, including the content class package that we previously created.

Content class package

First of all, we can make a content class package into which we can save the content class definition that we customized in the previous chapters.

The content class package is basically an archive containing all of the enhancement and personalization that we made to the CMF that can be exported to other eZ Publish installations.

To create a content class package, we have to:

1. Go to the backend site `http://packtmediaproject/index.php/ezwebin_ site_admin`.

2. Click on the **Setup** tab of top menu.

3. Click on the **Packages** link in left menu.

4. Click on the **Create new package** button.

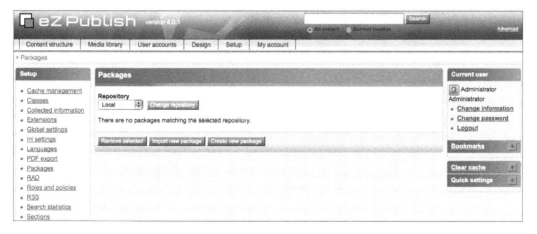

5.   Select the option button **Content class export**, and then click on the
     Create package button.

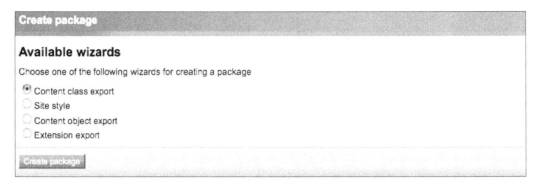

6.   Next, select the content classes **Article** and **Profile**, which we built in
     Chapter 3, from the class list. To continue, we have to click on the **Next** button.

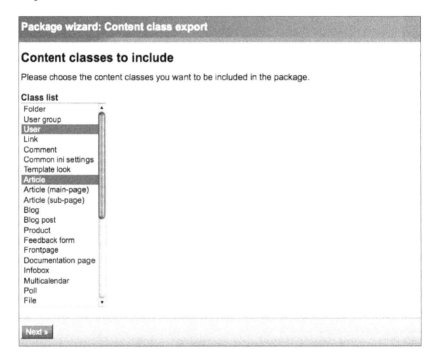

7. Next, we have to complete the form with information regarding the package that we are building, and then click on the **Next** button.

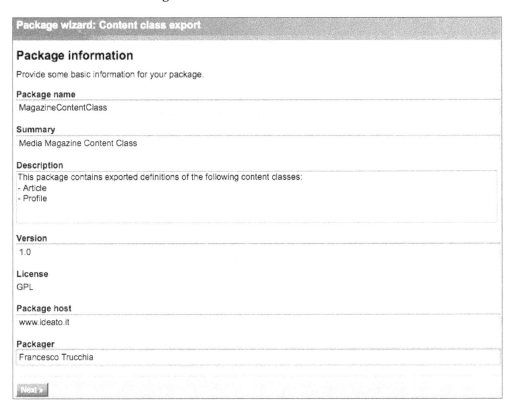

8. Specify the **Package maintainer** contents, and then click on the **Next** button.

9. As the last step, we will create a **changelog** with all the changes that we will add in this package release. Finally, we will click on the **Continue** button.

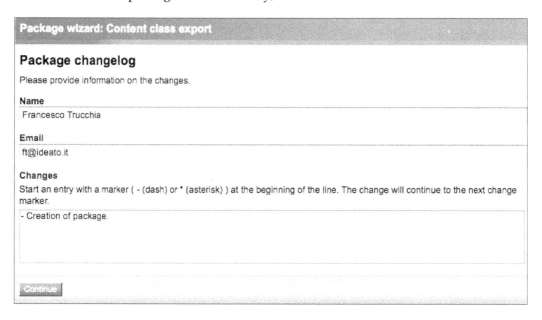

Our MagazineContentClass package is now ready. We can download it by clicking on the **Export to file** button and saving the file in an easily-accessible folder.

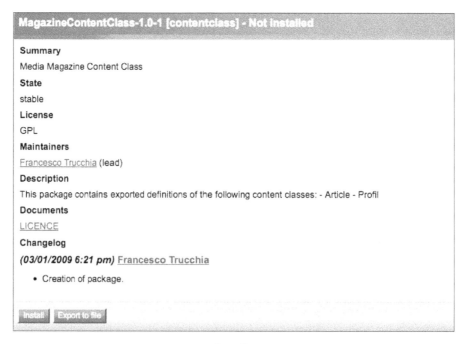

If we want to add this file to our extension to make our content class definition reusable and easily portable, we have to create a folder named `packages` in our extension and then add the downloaded file to this folder.

Open a shell and execute the following commands:

```
# cd /var/www/packtmediaproject/extension/packtmedia
# mkdir packages
# cp [browser_download_dir]/MagazineContentClass-1.0-1.ezpkg packages/
```

Now, when we will export our extension, it will include the content class package that we have created.

 The `.ezpkg` file is a compressed archive. We can uncompress it and see its contents with the `tar` command.

The first step to create our package is complete.

Extension packages

In this second step, we have to make our extension a package file.

As we can see, at the moment, the extension file is empty because our extension has only a folder structure. When we finish our job, we will need to carry out this step again, in order to have the complete extension.

To create an extension package, we need to follow the same steps that we saw earlier. The only change needed is when we have to choose the type of package to create, where we have to select the **Extension export** option button.

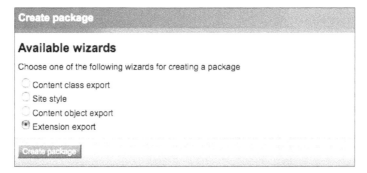

Next, we need to select the **packtmedia** option button, which is the extension that we want to export.

All of other steps are the same as for the Content Class package, and in the end, we can save this file in our computer. This file could be useful for re-using the same layout and extension in other projects, or to sell or distribute our extension.

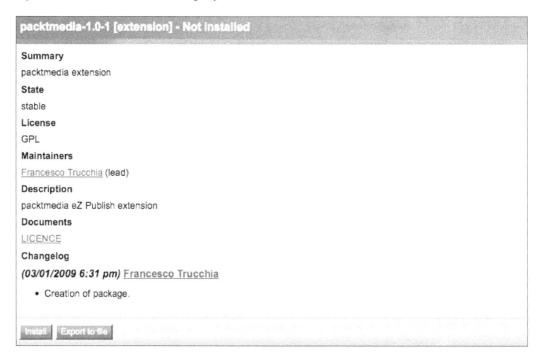

Business with extensions

Creating extensions for a project, as well as having an easy way to have code reusability, can also be a way to get more visibility in the eZ Publish community, or even to earn some money.

The eZ System, indeed, offers two ways to distribute an extension. The first way is through the website `http://projects.ez.no`. This site provides a platform for developers who want to release their extensions with an open source license. The site integrates:

- A news module
- A forum module
- A repository file system
- A versioning file system (SVN)

All of these services are free, but the staff at eZ System reserves the right to remove an extension if it is not considered suitable, or if it breaks the site guidelines.

Moreover, by distributing an extension with an open license, you can help the eZ Publish community get bigger, and you can get help in enhancing your own packages from the community.

The second way is accessible only to the partner companies of eZ System, and allows them to sell their extensions on the official site at `http://ez.no/software/certified_extensions`.

To ensure that an extension is certified, you must gain certification under the supervision of eZ System staff, and pay an annual fee for each extension that you want to re-sell. For more details, you can contact the eZ System company's support.

Summary

In this chapter, we learned how to build an extension to create our own custom layout, create new template operators, and have our translation files. We also learned how to create a package for a content class and for an extension.

We also saw how to export and import a package so that it can easily be re-used.

In the next chapter, we will see how to create a template design for the site, which will be added to our package.

6
Creating a Design

In the previous chapter, we learned how to place our code in a custom extension. In this chapter, we will learn how to manage our design in the same way. We will see what an eZ Publish template is and how to apply a template to a single content node or subtree. We will also take a look at template overrides and create a proper design extension starting from the eZ Webin package.

eZ Publish templating

In the first part of this chapter, we will introduce the basics of the eZ Publish templating system, which will help us to better understand the rest of this chapter and the next.

Templating

eZ Publish has its own templating system based on the decoupling of layout and content. This will help us to assign a custom layout to any content object in different sections.

Moreover, just as other templating platforms, such as Smarty (`http://www.smarty.net`), eZ Publish has its own markup to help developers with control structure operations, subtemplating, and on-the-fly content editing. It also exposes a particular function to fetch and filter content from a database.

 The official eZ Publish website has a constant, up-to-date reference with the entire templating markup. We suggest you to use the following link every time that you need to know more details about the available arguments:

`http://ez.no/doc/ez_publish/technical_manual/4_0/templates/`

The templating markup

All of the eZ Publish templating code should be placed between curly brackets ({ }). When the CMS will parse our template file and find the curly brackets, it will start executing the related code.

Escaping the curly brackets

If we need to use curly brackets, for example to write a `javascript` function inside our template, we need to use the `{literal}` operator.

```
{literal}
<script type="text/javascript">
function alertMe() {
    window.alert('Harkonen approaching!');
}
</script>
{/literal}
```

Control structure operators

We can divide these function into two main families:

- Conditional (IF-THEN-ELSE)
- Looping (FOR-FOREACH-WHILE)

Whereas the first one should be used to change the template behavior according to some predefined condition, the other one will help us to seek and manage array and content structures.

Conditional control

Conditional control is sometimes useful for changing the output when some data is received by the system. For example, we would need a different CSS class for a particular value, or to change the `<div>` class, if the current month is the same as the one displayed, as shown below:

```
{def $current_month=currentdate()|datetime(custom, '%F')}
{if $node.name|eq($current_month) }
<span class="this-month">
{else}
<span class="default-month">
{/if}
{undef $current_month}
```

In the first line, we define a `$current_month` variable that has a value of the name of the month (for example, *October*), retrieved by the `datetime()` operator. Then we use the `IF` conditional control to choose the correct class.

In the last line, we delete the variable previously created, by releasing it from system memory.

Loop control

As stated above, the loop control structure can be used to iterate through an array. We can, for example, create an unordered list (`<ul>`) from an array of items.

```
<ul>
{foreach $items as $item}
    <li>{node_view_gui content_node=$item view=line}</li>
{/foreach}
</ul>
```

This will be rendered as:

```
<ul>
    <li>1st item</li>
    <li>2nd item</li>
    <li>3rd item</li>
    ...
</ul>
```

As you can see, the `FOREACH` structure is similar to the PHP structure. In this example, the most interesting line is the definition of the list object. This we can literally read as: render the content node (`node_view_gui`) from a specific node (`content_node=$issue`) using the line view template (`view=line`).

Fetch functions

With the fetch functions, we can retrieve all of the information about a content object for a module. The fetch functions can also be used to create custom queries to retrieve only the information we need, and not everything.

eZ Publish exposes many fetch functions, which can be read about on the documentation site at `http://ez.no/doc/ez_publish/technical_manual/4_0/reference/template_fetch_functions`

The most important, and most used, fetch functions are those regarding the content, sections, and user modules. For example, we can fetch the root content object by using the following code in our template:

```
{$object = fetch('content', 'object', hash('id', '1'))}
```

We can then use the `$object` variable to display the object inside the HTML code.

Generic template functions and operators

The CMS gives us a lot of functions and operators, all of them described in the reference manual of the eZ System documentation site.

As a thumb rule, we should remember that to execute a particular function, we have to use the following syntax:

```
{function_name parameter1=value1 … parameterN=valueN }
```

All parameters are separated by spaces and can be specified in no particular order.

If we want to manage the operators, we have to remember that they accept the parameters passed in a specific order, separated by a comma. Moreover, an operator should handle a parameter passed to it with a pipe (|).

```
{$piped_parameter|my_operator( parameter1, …, parameterN ) }
```

Every time we see a pipe after a variable, we have to remember that we are passing a value to an operator.

We used the `datetime()` operator in the previous example for the conditional control functionality.

As a reference to API functions and operators, you can use the official variable documentation that is constantly updated on the eZ System site: http://ez.no/doc/ez_publish/technical_manual/4_0/reference/template_operators

http://ez.no/doc/ez_publish/technical_manual/4_0/reference/template_functions

Layout variables

By default, the page layout template can access some of the variables passed by the CMS. These variables, named Layout variables, can be used to render system and user information, or to change the output. These variables are automatically configured by eZ Publish when it analyzes and executes the code related to a view.

One of the most important variables is $module_result, which contains the results generated by the module and the view that is being executed.

A module is an HTTP interface that interacts with eZ Publish. A module consists of a set of views that contain the code to be executed. For example, if we call the following URL, the system executes the login view code of the user module: http://www.example.com/index.php/user/login.

As an API reference, you can use the official variable documentation that is constantly updated on the eZ System site: http://ez.no/doc/ez_publish/technical_manual/4_0/templates/the_pagelayout/variables_in_pagelayout

Overriding a template

eZ Publish offers a set of standard templates that are useful, but they cannot cover all the possible design needs.

To solve this issue, the CMF provides a fallback system that allows us to load different templates based on specific rules. This system is usually referred to as overriding, and allows us to change the template for each module's view by overriding the default template when the user is in a particular context.

Embedding HTML inside the WYSIWYG XML editor, pt.2

As we saw in Chapter 4, we had to override a standard behavior of eZ Publish to create a generic HTML block inside the WYSIWYG XML editor.

We previously created a content style named html for the online editor, but we didn't do anything for the frontend to render it correctly. Now, we will finish that work.

First, we have to create a file named `literal.tpl` and place it in the `design` folder of our extension. The following code will do exactly what we need:

```
# mkdir -p  /var/www/packtmediaproject/extension/packtmedia/design/
magazine/templates/datatype/view/ezxmltags/
```

```
# cd /var/www/packtmediaproject/extension/packtmedia/design/magazine/
templates/datatype/view/ezxmltags/
```

```
# touch literal.tpl
```

Next, we will open the `literal.tpl` file in our preferred IDE. Now we will add the code that will, by default, render everything surrounded by a `<pre>` tag and the raw HTML code, if the class is `html`:

```
{if ne( $classification, 'html' )}
    <pre {if ne( $classification|trim, '' )}
    class="{$classification|wash}"{/if}>{$content|wash( xhtml )}</pre>
{else}
    {$content}
{/if}
```

This code will check to see if the `$classification` variable is different from the "html" string in order to add the `<pre>` tag and then, again, it will add a class attribute to the `<pre>` tag if the `$classification` variable is not null.

To use it, we only need to reset the cache from the shell prompt by using the following command:

```
cd /var/www/packmediaproject/
```

```
php bin/php/ezcache.php --clear-all --purge
```

The `ezcache.php` file is a PHP shell script that can be used to clear and manage the eZ Publish cache. This file has many parameters, which can be viewed by using the `--help` parameter.

Creating a new design

Before starting work on the eZ Webin template code, we need to create a wireframe in order to decide on the layout structure. We will use this structure to override the standard layout files.

A wireframe is a basic visual guide that is used in web design to suggest the structure of a website and the relationships between its pages.

Wireframe editors

There are a lot of commercial and free wireframe editors. To create our site's wireframes, we will use the Firefox plugin called **Pencil** (`http://www.evolus.vn/Pencil/`).

We have chosen Pencil because it is open source and works on every platform that runs the Firefox browser.

If you need something more complete, you should take a look at **Balsamiq** (`http://www.balsamiq.com/`) or at **OmniGraffle** (`http://www.omnigroup.com/applications/OmniGraffle/`) if you have an Apple computer.

Our site will have at least six different page layouts:

- The **homepage**
- The **issue page**, where we will display the cover and the articles list
- The **issue archive** page, by month and by years
- The **staff profile page**, where we will display the latest articles that the editor has written, along with his profile
- The **article** and the **forum** pages, with the default layout based on the eZ Webin design

Now we will illustrate the first four layouts because we will work on them, overriding their standard eZ Webin layout. In Chapter 8, we will work on the forum and customize it to fulfill our future needs.

The homepage

Starting from the homepage, we can see that the site will have, in the top-left corner, a logo for the magazine and a place-holder for a banner. Under these, we will have the main navigation menu and the main content area.

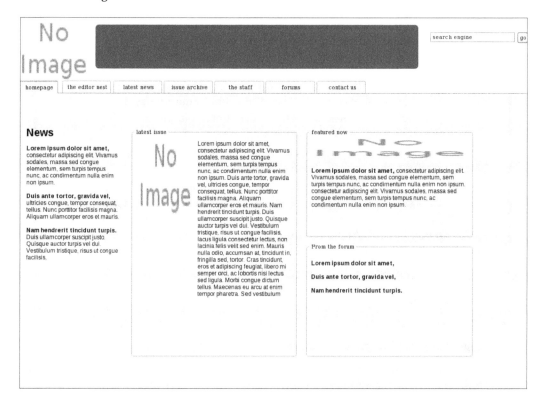

We have chosen a three-column layout in order to easily manage the content that we want to show.

In the **homepage**, the first column will show the latest news and the middle column will show the information and cover of the latest issue.

The last column will have two boxes — one with the most important article from the latest issue and the other with the forum thread.

Issue page

The **issue page** will show some information of a specific magazine issue.

In this page, the middle box of the homepage will shift towards the left, and in the right column there will be the highlighted article for the issue. At the bottom of the page, we will find all of the other articles.

The issue archive

We have to remember that our magazine is released monthly, so we need an archive page where we can collect all of the past issues.

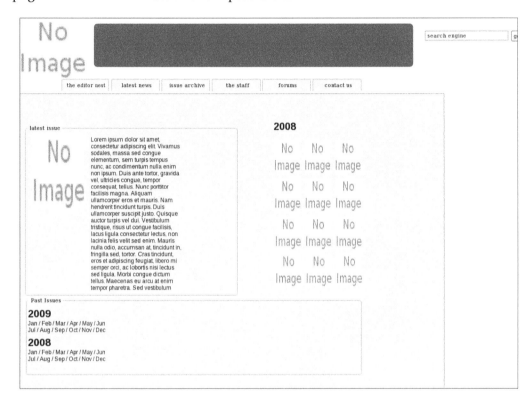

The **issue archive** page, which can be reached by clicking on the main navigation menu, will again show some information from the latest issue. (We need to sell our articles!)

The rightmost column of the template will show all of the covers for the current or selected year.

At the bottom of the page, we will create a box with links to the past issues grouped by years and months.

The staff profile page

The staff profile page will display information from a staff profile, such as his avatar, biography, and the latest articles that he has written.

The **staff profile page** will have three columns. The first column will show information regarding the editor's profile, the middle column will show all of the articles the editor has written (paged five by five) and the third will be used for banners or other images.

eZ Webin

In Chapter 1, we installed the eZ Webin package as a sample frontend for our site. This package is very flexible and is usually used as a starting point for developing a new site. By default, it includes:

- A flexible layout
- Some useful custom content classes (blog, event, forum, article, and so on)
- Web 2.0 features, such as a tag cloud and comment functions
- Custom template operators

In our project, we will extend and override the eZ Webin template in order to create the Packtmedia Magazine site and add some features needed for the project. We will see this step-by-step as we understand better how eZ Publish works.

Overriding the standard page layout

The page layout is the main template and defines the style of the entire site. To create a page layout template, we need to create a file named `pagelayout.tpl` and place it inside the `templates` folder of our design extension.

As we said, we will work with eZ Webin. This extension doesn't use the standard page layout but overrides the standard page layout with its own custom behavior. We need to do the same overriding from the eZ Webin `pagelayout.tpl`.

To override the template, we have to copy it in our design's `extension` folder placed in `extension/packtmedia/design/magazine/templates/`. Now open a shell and execute this:

```
# cd /var/www/packtmediaproject/extension
# cp /ezwebin/design/ezwebin/templates/pagelayout.tpl /packtmedia/
design/magazine/templates/
```

We will use this new `pagelayout.tpl` file to implement the wireframe that we developed in the previous sections.

Section for our project

eZ Publish includes features for creating a particular view in order to add content objects inside specified sections. For example, if we take a look at our wireframe, we need to assign a different layout for rendering the `Issue archive` folder and its subfolders.

To do this, we have to create a new section in the administration panel and associate it to the entire **Issue archive** subtree. After that, we can use the fetch functions to select the correct view for that section.

Creating a new section

To create a new section, we have to open our browser and from the site's backend, select the **Setup** tab from the top menu. We then need to navigate to the **Sections** link in the left-hand menu, and then click on the **New section** button.

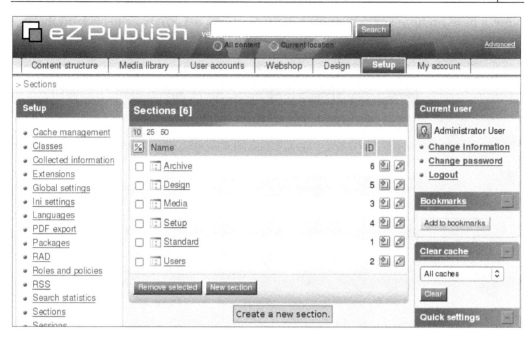

Next, we will create a new section called **Archive** and select the default **Content structure** value in the select menu.

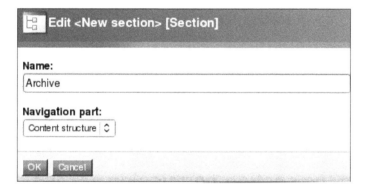

Now, a new **Archive** link will appear in the **Sections** list. We have to click on the + button to the left of the **Archive** link, and then select the **Issue archive** node, by selecting the relevant checkbox.

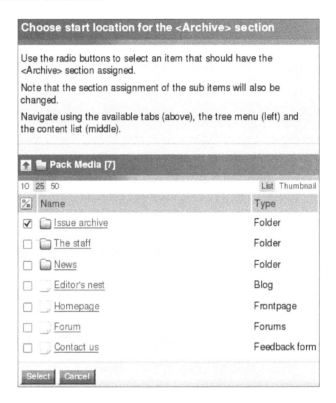

After we have saved, click on the **Select** button. All of the **Issue archive** subfolders will be placed inside the **Archive** section. We have to remember the ID of this section, which we'll use to create the override rules. In this case, the section ID number is **6**, as seen in the first screenshot in the *Creating a new section* section.

Setting up the section permission access

By default, eZ Publish creates private sections that only an administrator can access. To make a section public, we need to give read permission to anonymous users.

To set up the rules, we have to go back to **Setup** tab on the top menu, and then click on the **Role and policies** link on the left-hand menu.

Here, we have to click on the **Edit** button on the right-hand side of the **Anonymous** link, and then click on the **New policy** button.

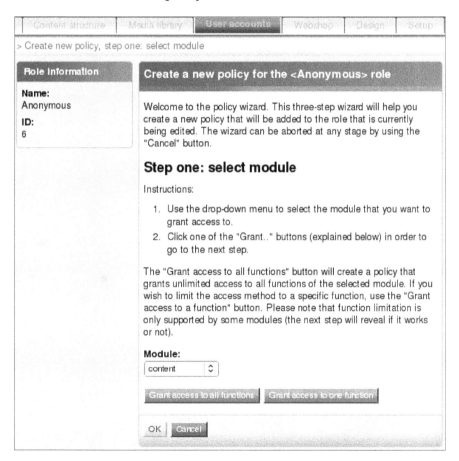

Next, select the **content** option in the **Module** field, and then click on the **Grant access to one function** button.

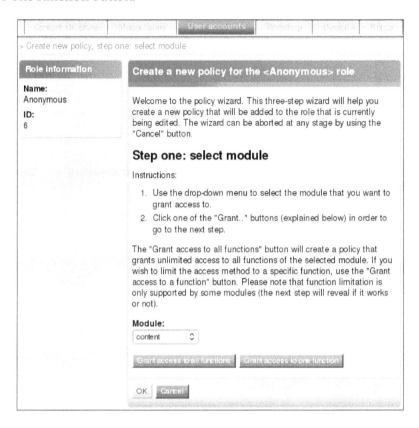

Select the **read** option in the **Function** field, and then click on the **Grant limited access** button.

Next, select the **Archive** option for the **Section** field. Click on the **OK** button, and then click on the **OK** button on the **Edit <Anonymous> Role** page.

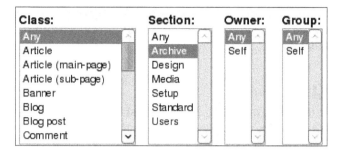

Now, the anonymous user can access the **Archive** section.

In the next paragraph, we will use this section to create custom override rules.

Customizing the page layout

After we copy the pagelayout.tpl template into the new path, we have to work on it in order to create the three columns inside the content layout of the eZ Webin template.

To do this, first of all, we have to remove the leftmost sidebar, along with the secondary navigation menu, inside the **Archive** section that we have created.

Open the pagelayout.tpl file that you have copied into your favorite IDE, and take a look at the code.

At line 62 we will find the following code:

```
{if and( is_set( $content_info.class_identifier ), ezini(
'MenuSettings', 'HideLeftMenuClasses', 'menu.ini' )|contains(
$content_info.class_identifier ) )}
    {set $pagestyle = 'nosidemenu noextrainfo'}
```

Here, eZ Webin hides the side menu if the content class belongs to the array returned by the ezini operator.

We now need to extend the IF sentence and add a control to the section ID, by using the following code:

```
{if or(and( is_set( $content_info.class_identifier ), ezini(
'MenuSettings', 'HideLeftMenuClasses', 'menu.ini' )|contains(
$content_info.class_identifier ) ), $module_result.section_id|eq(6))}
    {set $pagestyle = 'nosidemenu noextrainfo'}
```

As we can see, this code will now check to see if the browsed section has an ID equal to 6 (that is, the achive section ID that we previously created) and if it has, will hide the unnecessary sidebar.

CSS editing

Luckily, the entire template code of eZ Webin is strongly semantic and all of the elements have their own IDs and classes. Thanks to this, we can change a lot of things by simply working on the CSS.

By default, the CMS uses six CSSes. These are:

- `core.css`: this is the global stylesheet where all of the standard tag styles for eZ Publish are defined; usually, this file is overridden by all of the others

- `webstyletoolbar.css`: this stylesheet is imported for the frontend web toolbar that is used for editing the content

- `pagelayout.css`: this is where all of the default styles of the global pagelayout are defined

- `content.css`: this is where all the default styles of the content classes are defined

- `site-colors.css`: this file is used to override the `pagelayout.css` to skin a site differently

- `classes-colors.css`: this file is used to override the default styles defined by the `content.css` file

To edit the CSS, we have to copy the original eZ Webin stylesheet from the `/var/www/packtmediaproject/extension/ezwebin/design/ezwebin/stylesheets` folder to our `design` directory and then to execute the following commands:

```
# cd /var/www/packtmediaproject/extension/
# cp -rf ezwebin/design/ezwebin
/stylesheets/*  packtmedia/design/magazine/stylesheets/
```

Now, every time that we want to change the stylesheet, we have to remember to edit the CSS files in the `design/magazine/stylesheets/` directory of our extension.

Creating a new style package

In eZ Publish, as we did for extension, it's possible to create a portable style package, so we can share and reuse our custom style in other sites. We can do this by navigating to the backend admin site and uploading the new stylesheet that we want to use.

First, we have to create our CSS files by using our favorite CSS editor; we have to remember that they will override the default styles, so we only need to add the lines that we want to change.

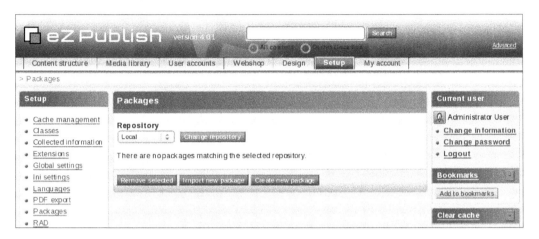

After we create the new stylesheet files, we have to open the browser, click on the **Setup** tab, and then click on the **Package** link in the left-hand sidebar.

The system will ask us where we want to create our new package.

We will select the local repository and click on the **Create new package** button. eZ Publish will then ask us which kind of package we want to create. We have to select the **Site style** wizard, and then click on the **Create new package** button.

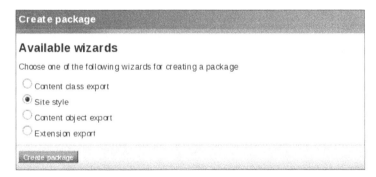

We can now choose a thumbnail for the style that we are uploading, or continue without it.

After selecting the thumbnail, the wizard will ask us to choose the CSS file that we previously created. Select it, and then click on the **Next** button.

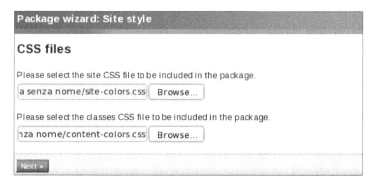

With the wizard, we will also upload one or more images, for example a new logo file, or other images related to the CSS. To not upload files, we simply have to click on the **Next** button without selecting a file in the form.

 We have to remember that all of the images that we upload will be saved in a subfolder named `images`, which will be placed in the same directory as the stylesheet. This will be useful when we need to set the relative path of the images used inside the CSS.

We can now add the package information, just as we did in Chapter 5, and export it to our PC (if required).

The new style package will automatically be installed in the eZ Publish package folder. It will be accessible from the **Design** tab, via the sidebar's **Look and Feel** link.

If we select the package and clear the cache automatically, it will be applied to the frontend.

Summary

In this chapter, we learned the basics of the templating system of eZ Publish. We worked on template's function and operator, and also learned how to extend the default WYSIWYG editor of eZ Publish.

Moreover, we created the site wireframe and learned how the design overriding feature works.

We also created a new stylesheet package, and applied it to our extension. In the next chapter, we will create a custom template for all of the content classes that we created previously.

7
Template Content Class

Separating presentation from business logic

– Model View Controller Pattern

In this chapter, we'll see how it's possible to customize our custom class views through the override system and the template engine.

Introduction to the content template

In the previous chapter, we saw that eZ Publish offers an out of the box template standard set. With this set of templates, it's possible to render all of the system module views correctly.

There are two template types. The first is the content template, which is used from every system module. For example, the view to see the items list of feed module. The second is the "node system template", which is used by the content module to see the object content published on the tree. This template is very important because the "content" module is the main module of the system. This module manages all of the actions on the object, such as publishing, moving, coping, deleting, and so on. It also manages the override system, through which it is possible to override the standard view for each rendered object.

We'll use the "node template" for our custom classes, and we'll also override the standard template without using custom templates.

The system provides different views for each node. By node, we mean the node of the content tree to which a content object or an instance of some class is associated.

For example, if we create a page staff below the staff node in our content tree, we can create different templates for this page (the object assigned to a node), so that it can be viewed in different ways, depending on where it will be rendered.

This feature is possible because we can explicitly tell the system which view is to be use to render a given content node.

For example, if we go to `http://packtmediaproject/eng/content/view/full/74`, we can see the node with ID 74 in its full view. Alternatively, if we go to `http://packtmediaproject/eng/content/view/line/74`, we can see the node with ID 74, but in its line view.

It's also possible to force the rendered content view of a content node through the {node_view_gui} template function, by passing a "view" parameter with the specific view string.

For example:

{node_view_gui view=full content_node=74} will render the "full" view of the node with ID 74.

and

{node_view_gui view=line content_node=74} will render the "line" view of the node with ID 74.

eZ Publish already covers some types of view, such as full and line for the standard classes, with some standard templates. But if the view does not meet the standard requirements, or if we need to create a custom view for our custom classes, we must create a rule to override these views.

The override system

The override system is able to load different kinds of content node views instead of the standard view, based on defined rules.

Creating a template override

In our project, we can override the standard views for the following standard and custom classes:

- Class Profile with full, line, and embed views
- Class Folder for the "Issue Year" section with a full view
- Class Folder for the "Issues" section with thumb, full, line, and embed views
- Class Folder for the "Issue Archive" section with full and embed views
- Class Article with full, line, and embed views

Usually, the full view is used to view a content node with all of its attributes. (We can think of a full content node view as a static HTML page of that element.) The line view is used to view the content node in a list, for example, if we want to see all articles published in a given year. The embed view is used if we want to attach a content node to another content node description attribute.

To create our override rules, we can use an automatic method through the graphic eZ Publish interface, or we can add rules manually to the `override.ini.append.php` file of each siteaccess where we want to render the custom view instead of the standard view.

Creating a template override from a graphic interface

Through the graphical interface of eZ Publish, you can create rules in the `override.ini` file. Unfortunately, this interface is very limited and not very usable, which is why we prefer to create rules and files manually. The limitations of creating rules through the interface are many. First of all, you cannot specify all of the rules allowed by the file that is being overridden, and it is also not possible to structure the override files into a well-ordered folder tree. All files are placed inside the override templates of our design extension. If we override many files, you will appreciate that it becomes very difficult to maintain the folder order.

Let's see one example of how you can create an override of the class folder for the section with ID 6, which corresponds to our **Issue archive**. In the next section, we'll see in detail how to manually create all of the template overrides along with their rules.

To create a new override rule, we need to log into the site backend and fill the user login form with our credentials.

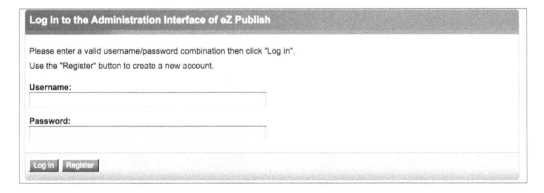

Next, we need to select the **Design** tab on the top menu, and then click on the **Template** link in the leftmost menu.

Now we are on the page where we can see a list of all system templates and override templates. Below this, we can also see a list of the M**ost common templates**.

Most common templates	
Template	Design resource
/node/view/line.tpl	extension/ezwebin/design/ezwebin/templates
/node/view/text_linked.tpl	design/standard/templates
/node/view/embed.tpl	extension/ezwebin/design/ezwebin/templates
/node/view/objectrelationlist.tpl	design/standard/templates
/node/view/full.tpl	extension/ezwebin/design/ezwebin/templates
/node/view/listitem.tpl	design/standard/templates
/node/view/embed-inline.tpl	design/standard/templates
/node/view/thumb.tpl	design/standard/templates
/node/view/execute_pdf.tpl	design/standard/templates
/node/view/pdf.tpl	design/standard/templates
/node/view/toolline.tpl	design/standard/templates
/node/view/plain.tpl	design/standard/templates
/node/view/sitemap.tpl	extension/ezwebin/design/ezwebin/templates
/node/view/text.tpl	design/standard/templates
/node/view/search.tpl	design/standard/templates
/toolbar/line/basket.tpl	design/standard/templates
/toolbar/full/basket.tpl	design/standard/templates
/shop/basket.tpl	extension/ezwebin/design/ezwebin/templates
/content/view/embed.tpl	design/standard/templates
/content/view/embed-inline.tpl	design/standard/templates
/content/advancedsearch.tpl	extension/ezwebin/design/ezwebin/templates

We want to override the content node view, **full**, for the Folder class. So, we must click on **/node/view/full.tpl** in the **Most common templates** list.

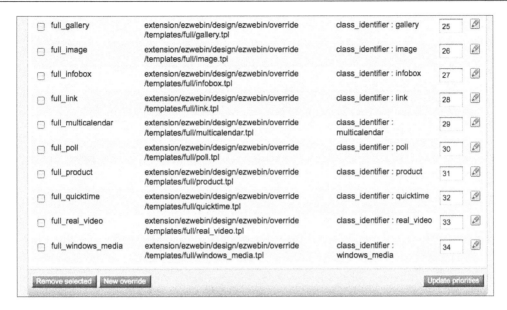

The page that is now loaded, has all the template override rule settings for the standard template /node/view/full.tpl. To create a new template, we need to click on the **New override** button at the bottom of the list.

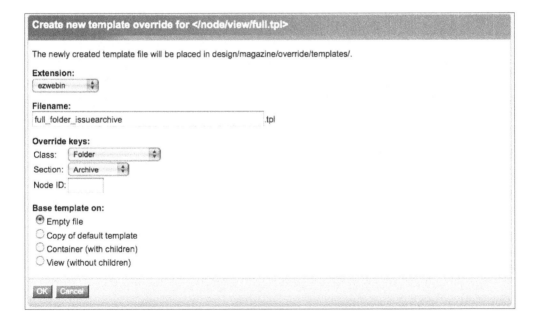

The page that is loaded has a form in which we have to specify the following information:

- **Filename** (the system suggests specifying an explanatory name)
- **Class** for which we are adding this override
- **Section** for which we are doing this override
- **Node ID**, if the override is only for a specific content node

We also need to choose if we want to create an **Empty file**, a copy of the original standard template, a container, or a simple view.

In our situation, we name the file **full_folder_issuearchive.tpl**. We select the **Folder** class and the **Archive** section, as created in the previous chapter, to manage this rule. At the end, we choose to create an **Empty file**, and then click on the **OK** button. Now our override rule and file are created.

A new override rule is always put at the end of the rule list. The system loads the first file where the rules match the context. So for this override, we have to increase the priority value from **35** to **1**. To do this, we have to change the value in the form field, which is in the column before the **edit** button, and click on the **Update priorities** button.

By clicking on the **Edit** button, it is possible to modify the template source code. If we have a template (it could be an idea) with very complex code inside it, it could be impossible to manage the template with this feature because the textarea does not support code highlight and indentation. It would be better to use our favorite IDE to edit it.

As you can see, the automatic override mechanism is not simple to use. We recommend that you manually create the rules and provide order to the files in your override folder.

Creating a template override manually

As we want to create custom views only for the frontend siteaccess, we need to change the override.ini.append.php file within the settings folder for all of our siteaccesses:

- /var/www/packtmediaproject/settings/siteaccess/ezwebin_site/
  override.ini.append.php

- /var/www/packtmediaproject/settings/siteaccess/ita/override.ini.append.php
- /var/www/packtmediaproject/settings/siteaccess/eng/override.ini.append.php
- /var/www/packtmediaproject/settings/siteaccess/fre/override.ini.append.php
- /var/www/packtmediaproject/settings/siteaccess/dev/ override.ini.append.php
- /var/www/packtmediaproject/settings/siteaccess/staging/override.ini.append.php"

Because the file will always be the same for all four siteaccess, it would be useful to change only one, for example the `siteaccess ezwebin_site` file, and then create a symbolic link to the master file within the other three siteaccess.

```
# cd /var/www/packtmediaproject/settings/siteaccess
# rm -r ita/override.ini.append.php eng/override.ini.append.php fre/
override.ini.append.php dev/override.ini.append.php staging/override.ini.
append.php
# ln -s  ezwebin_site/override.ini.append.php ita/
# ln -s  ezwebin_site/override.ini.append.php eng/
# ln -s  ezwebin_site/override.ini.append.php fre/
# ln -s ezwebin_site/override.ini.append.php dev/
#ln -s ezwebin_site/override.ini.append.php staging/"
```

Profile class

We will write the following rule in the file to create the `full` view for the `Profile` class:

```
[profile_full]
Source=node/view/full.tpl
MatchFile=full/profile.tpl
Subdir=templates
Match[class_identifier]=editor_profile
```

We will write the following rule in the file under the `[profile_full]` rule to create the `line` view for the `Profile` class:

```
[profile_line]
Source=node/view/line.tpl
MatchFile=line/profile.tpl
Subdir=templates
Match[class_identifier]=editor_profile
```

We will write the following rule under the `[profile_line]` rule in the file to create the `embed` view for the `Profile` class:

```
[profile_embed]
Source=node/view/embed.tpl
MatchFile=embed/profile.tpl
Subdir=templates
Match[class_identifier]=editor_profile
```

The section name should be unique within the `override.ini.append.php` file. The `Source` is the position in which the source file that we want to override is placed. The `MatchFile` is the location where you will find our custom file, starting from `Subdir`, which is the subdirectory override folder from the extension of our design. For example, to view `profile_full`, we want to overwrite the standard file `node/view/full.tpl` with our file override `templates/full/profile.tpl` only if the identifier of the class is equal to `profile`.

Folder class for the issue year archive

We will write the following rule, under the `[profile_embed]` rule, in the file to create the `full` view for the `folder` class in the **issue year archive**:

```
[folder_issueyear]
Source=node/view/full.tpl
MatchFile=full/folder_issueyear.tpl
Subdir=templates
Match[class_identifier]=folder
Match[section]=6
Match[depth]=3
```

Folder class for issue

We will write the following rule, under the `[folder_issueyear]` rule, in the file to create the `full` view for the `folder` class and render our **issue** page:

```
[folder_issue_full]
Source=node/view/full.tpl
MatchFile=full/folder_issue.tpl
Subdir=templates
Match[class_identifier]=folder
Match[parent_class]=folder
Match[section]=6
Match[depth]=4
```

We will write the following rule, under the `[folder_issue_full]` rule, in the file to create the `line` view for the `folder` class and render our **issue** page:

```
[folder_issue_line]
Source=node/view/line.tpl
MatchFile=line/folder_issue.tpl
Subdir=templates
Match[class_identifier]=folder
Match[parent_class]=folder
Match[section]=6
Match[depth]=4
```

We will write the following rule, under the `[folder_issue_line]` rule, in the file to create the `embed` view for the `folder` class and render our **issue** page:

```
[folder_issue_embed]
Source=node/view/embed.tpl
MatchFile=embed/folder_issue.tpl
Subdir=templates
Match[class_identifier]=folder
Match[parent_class]=folder
Match[section]=6
Match[depth]=4
```

We will write the following rule, under the `[folder_issue_embed]` rule, in the file to create the `thumb` view for the `folder` class and render our **issue** page:

```
[folder_issue_thumb]
Source=node/view/thumb.tpl
MatchFile=thumb/folder_issue.tpl
Subdir=templates
Match[class_identifier]=folder
Match[parent_class]=folder
Match[section]=6
Match[depth]=4
```

The `Match[depth]` rule matches the node with a depth equal to 4 in the content tree nodes.

Folder class for the issue archive section

We will write the following rule, under the [folder_issue_thumb] rule, in the file to create the full view for the folder class in the **issue archive** section:

```
[folder_issuearchive_full]
Source=node/view/full.tpl
MatchFile=full/folder_issuearchive.tpl
Subdir=templates
Match[class_identifier]=folder
# the Archive id section created in the previuos chapter
Match[section]=6
```

We will write the following rule, under the [folder_issuearchive_full] rule, in the file to create the embed view for the folder class in the **issue archive** section:

```
[folder_issuearchive_embed]
Source=node/view/embed.tpl
MatchFile=embed/folder_issuearchive.tpl
Subdir=templates
Match[class_identifier]=folder
Match[section]=6
```

Article class

We will write the following rule, under the [folder_issuearchive_embed] rule, in the file to create the full view for the article class and render the article items inside our issue:

```
[issue_article_full]
Source=node/view/full.tpl
MatchFile=full/issue_article.tpl
Subdir=templates
Match[class_identifier]=article
Match[section]=6
```

We will write the following rule, under the [issue_article_full] rule, in the file to create the line view for the article class:

```
[issue_article_line]
Source=node/view/line.tpl
MatchFile=line/issue_article.tpl
Subdir=templates
Match[class_identifier]=article
Match[section]=6
```

We will write the following rule, under the `[issue_article_line]` rule, in the file to create the `embed` view for the `article` class:

```
[issue_article_embed]
Source=node/view/embed.tpl
MatchFile=embed/issue_article.tpl
Subdir=templates
Match[class_identifier]=article
Match[section]=6
```

Frontpage embed object

For the home page, we'll use the standard class eZ Webin called **FrontPage**, which gives us the opportunity to have a layout with three columns. This also satisfies the needs of our mockup. Within the three columns, we need different types of boxes to represent:

- The left column:
  - The latest news
- The central column:
  - The latest issue
- The right column:
  - The most important article for the week
  - The latest item from the forum

To create these boxes, we'll use the standard eZ Webin templates to embed objects using the existing override. This can be activated by selecting the correct class for the embed object.

To meet our needs, we must modify the following two files for the extension eZ Webin:

- `extension/ezwebin/desing/ezwebin/override/templates/embed/vertically_listed_sub_items.tpl`
- `extension/ezwebin/desing/ezwebin/override/templates/itemizedsubitems/folder.tpl`

We must copy them into our extension in the same location.

Creating our custom template file

Finally, we must create our custom files for each rule of the override:

```
# cd /var/www/packtmediaproject/extension/packtmedia/design/magazine/
override/templates

# mkdir full line embed thumb itemizedsubitems

# touch full/profile.tpl line/profile.tpl embed/profile.tpl

# touch full/folder_issuearchive.tpl embed/folder_issuearchive.tpl

# touch full/folder_issue.tpl line/folder_issue.tpl embed/folder_issue.
tpl thumb/folder_issue.tpl

# touch full/issue_article.tpl line/issue_article.tpl embed/issue_
article.tpl

# touch full/feedbackform.tpl

# cp ../../../../ezwebin/design/ezwebin/override/templates/embed/
vertically_listed_sub_items.tpl embed/

#cp ../../../../ezwebin/desing/ezwebin/override/templates/
itemizedsubitems/folder.tpl  itemizedsubitems
```

Customizing our class templates

After creating our template files, it is time to edit the HTML and logic, in order to create our own custom classes (profile) and standard classes (folder, article) views in the **issue** section that will have a different appearance to the standard layout.

Now, we will look at the code of most complex classes, according to the override rules that we previously created.

Staff profile template

For the **Staff** class, we'll have two main views: the line view and the full view. We can start from the **line** view template.

Line template

To modify the template, we must open the `extension/packtmedia/design/magazine/override/templates/line/profile.tpl` file, and add the following code:

```
<div class="content-view-line">
  <div class="class-profile">
  <h2>
    <a href={$node.url_alias|ezurl} title="{$node.name}">
      {attribute_view_gui attribute=$node.data_map.firstname}
```

```
        {attribute_view_gui attribute=$node.data_map.lastname}
      </a>
    </h2>
    {attribute_view_gui attribute=$node.data_map.photo
                        alignment=left
                        image_class=small
                        css_class=profile
                        href=$node.url_alias}
  {$node.data_map.profile_description.content.output.output_
  text|striptags|shorten(200, '…')}
    </div>
</div>
```

$node is the variable that eZ Publish will make available within the content template. It is an ezcontentobjecttreenode object type. This variable contains information about the object that we are rendering and its associated node (position, depth, URL, and so on).

The $node.url_alias attribute prints the relative URL of the node. We can obtain the node's absolute path by appending the ezurl operator.

The $node.name attribute gives the object name and it's a proxy attribute to $node.object.name. The string rendered is the string defined in the **Object name pattern** when we define the class content.

With the attribute_view_gui function, we'll see the subtemplate related to a specific content object attribute. For example, with {attribute_view_gui attribute=$node.data_map.firstname}, we can see the subtemplate related to the firstname content object attribute of the ezstring type that is defined in the profile class. The $node.data_map attribute is a proxy attribute of the $node.object.data_map attribute. It is an array containing all attribute values of an object defined in our custom class.

All template attributes are located in the design/standard/templates/content/datatype/view/ folder, and can be overridden in our extension by copying the file to the same location as the original.

For example, if we want to override the ezstring attribute, we must copy the design/standard/templates/content/datatype/view/ezstring.tpl file to the extension/packtmedia/design/magazine/templates/content/datatype/view/ezstring.tpl file, and then clear the cache so that the system loads the custom file rather than the standard one. Now you can edit the custom file, and each time that the system loads the template related to the ezstring attribute, it will load our new file.

With the {attribute_view_gui attribute=$node.data_map.lastname} function, we can render the lastname object attribute defined as ezstring.

```
{attribute_view_gui attribute=$node.data_map.photo
                     alignment=left
                     image_class=small
                     css_class=profile
                     href=$node.url_alias}
```

With this function, we can render the photo object attribute defined as ezimage. Because the datatype ezimage is a more complex datatype, we can pass multiple parameters to the function in order to correctly display the image.

With the alignment parameter, we define the alignment of the image. This parameter accepts the left, right, and center values.

With the image_class parameter, we pass the alias that defines the size of the image and filters to be used, if defined. These aliases are defined in the file image.ini.

With the css_class parameter, we pass a class style that comes loaded in the attribute class of the img tag.

With the href parameter, we can make the image clickable, and the value passed is the address of the link.

With the {$node.data_map.profile_description.content.output.output_text|striptags|shorten(200, '...')} code, we'll render the first 200 characters of the description attribute. The $node.data_map.profile_description.content.output.output_text attribute contains the output of the ezxmltext attribute named description. With the striptags operator, we strip all of the HTML tags from output and with the shorten operator, we take the first 200 characters of the string.

Whereas the shorten operator is a standard eZ Publish operator, the striptags operator isn't. In eZ Publish, we can call back the standard PHP function, which takes only one parameter as input. It is sufficient to create an override of the template.ini setting file in the settings folder of our extension, call template.ini.append.php file, and then insert the following code:

```php
<?php /*

[PHP]
PHPOperatorList[striptags]=strip_tags

*/ ?>
```

The PHPOperatorList array key is the operator name, whereas the value is the name of the PHP function.

The result of this custom view is as follows:

Full template

To modify the template, we must open the `extension/packtmedia/design/`
`magazine/override/templates/full/profile.tpl` file and add the following
code to it:

```
{def $latest_articles=fetch(content, reverse_related_objects,
                hash('object_id', $node.object.id,
                     'attribute_identifier', '345',
                     'all_relations', true(),
                     'sort_by', array( 'published', false() ) ))}
<div class="content-view-full">
    <div class="profile-full">
        <div class="info">
            <div class="border-box">
                <div class="border-tl">
                    <div class="border-tr">
                        <div class="border-tc"></div>
                    </div>
                </div>
                <div class="border-ml">
                    <div class="border-mr">
                        <div class="border-mc float-break">
        <h1>{$node.name|wash}</h1>
        {attribute_view_gui attribute=$node.data_map.photo
```

```
                              alignment=left
                              image_class=medium
                              css_class=profile}
          {attribute_view_gui
                              attribute=$node.data_map.profile_description}
                </div>
              </div>
            </div>
            <div class="border-bl">
                <div class="border-br">
                    <div class="border-bc"></div>
                </div>
            </div>
          </div>
        </div>
        <div class="articles">
            <div class="border-box">
              <div class="border-tl">
                  <div class="border-tr">
                      <div class="border-tc"></div>
                  </div>
              </div>
              <div class="border-ml">
                  <div class="border-mr">
                      <div class="border-mc float-break">
        <h1>{'Latest articles'|i18n('design/packtmedia')}</h1>
        {foreach $latest_articles as $article}
          {node_view_gui content_node=$article.main_node view=line}
        {/foreach}
                      </div>
                  </div>
              </div>
              <div class="border-bl">
                  <div class="border-br">
                      <div class="border-bc"></div>
                  </div>
              </div>
            </div>
        </div>
    </div>
</div>
```

This template is a bit more complex than the previous one. Now we'll look at the various code parts used.

```
{def $latest_articles=fetch(content, reverse_related_objects,
            hash('object_id', $node.object.id,
                    'attribute_identifier', '345',
                    'all_relations', true(),
                    'sort_by', array( 'published', false() ) ))}
```

This code is used to retrieve articles written by the author. The `def` function defines a new variable inside the template. The `fetch` function is a simple way to query the database. For example, in this case, the fetch function calls the `reverse_related_objects` function of the content module. It is used to retrieve all of the elements related indirectly to a certain node. In our case, the elements are the objects related to the attribute with an ID of `345`. Here, we retrieve all of the articles related indirectly to the **profile** content object.

As with the line view, we show the name, photo, and description of the author and, finally, the code:

```
<h1>{'Latest articles'|i18n('design/packtmedia')}</h1>
{foreach $latest_articles as $article}
   {node_view_gui content_node=$article.main_node view=line}
{/foreach}
```

Here, we display the articles related to the author. The `i18n` operator is used to load the localized string as is appropriate. We will see this feature in detail in Chapter 9.

In the `foreach` function, we loop through the `$latest_articles` array and render the `line` view of each node, by calling the `node_view_gui` function.

The result of this custom view is as follows:

Embed template

To modify the template, we need to open the `extension/packtmedia/design/ magazine/override/templates/embed/profile.tpl` file, and add the following code to it:

```
<div class="content-view-full">
    <div class="class-profile">
        {$node.name|wash}
    </div>
</div>
```

Through this template, we simply display the name of the author.

Issue template

Now, we will look at the views for the folder that represents our "issue".

Line template

To modify the template, we need to open the `extension/packtmedia/design/ magazine/override/templates/line/folder_issue.tpl` file, and add the following code to it:

```
<div class="content-view-line">
    <div class="line-folder-issue">
        <h2><a href={$node.url_alias|ezurl}>{$node.name}</a></h2>
        {include uri="design:parts/issue/entrymeta.tpl" node=$node}
    <div class="entrybody">
        {attribute_view_gui attribute=$node.data_map.cover
                            alignment=left
                            image_class=small
                            css_class=profile
                            href=$node.url_alias|ezurl(no) }
        {attribute_view_gui
                            attribute=$node.data_map.short_description}
    </div>
        {include uri="design:parts/issue/authors.tpl" node=$node}
    </div>
</div>
```

In this template, as with the previous templates, we want to render the object name through the {$node.name} code, the object link through the {$node.url_alias|ezurl} attribute, the issue code through the {attribute_view_gui attribute=$node.data_map.cover...} function, and the description through the {attribute_view_gui attribute=$node.data_map.short_description} function.

Furthermore, in the template, we also want to see the list of authors who have written for this issue. For this block, we include a sub-template, as the same code is also used in other templates. To include it in this template, we must use the {include uri = "design:parts/issue/authors.tpl" node=$node}. The uri parameter specifies template to be loaded; all subsequent parameters are variables that are passed to the template. In this case, the template will load the extension/packtmedia/design/magazine/templates/parts/issue/authors.tpl template file.

The authors.tpl template should contain the following code:

```
{def $found=array()}
<h2>{"Authors on this issue"|i18n('design/magazine')}</h2>
<ul>
{foreach $node.children as $child}
    {if is_set($child.data_map.author_profile)}
        {foreach $child.data_map.author_profile.content.relation_list
          as $related}
            {if $found|contains($related.node_id)|not}
                {set $found=$found|append($related.node_id)}
                <li>{node_view_gui content_node=fetch('content', 'node',
                                    hash('node_id', $related.node_id))
                                 view=text_linked}</li>
            {/if}
        {/foreach}
    {/if}
{/foreach}
</ul>
{undef $found}
```

The code of this template is rather complex. In eZ Publish, retrieving a certain datatype (in this case, all of the authors relate to individual items within an issue) is not easy, and we are forced to create a lot of logic. There are alternatives to create a less-complex logic, such as creating custom PHP functions and using its template. In this case, we chose to utilize the logic of the template because the caching mechanism speeds up the loading of a complex page.

The result of this custom view is:

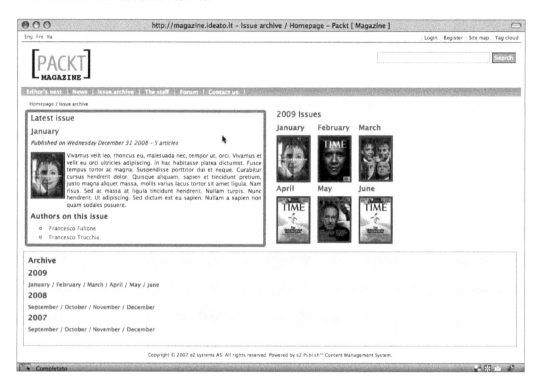

Full template

To modify the template, we need to edit the `extension/packtmedia/design/magazine/override/templates/full/folder_issue.tpl` file, and add the following code to it:

```
{def $folder = fetch(content, list,
                hash('parent_node_id', $node.node_id,
                    'limit', 1,
                    'class_filter_type', 'include',
                    'class_filter_array', array('folder')))}
<div class="content-view-full">
    <div class="folder-issuearhive-full">
        <div class="info" {if is_set($folder.0)|not}style="width:
                        100%"{/if}>
            <div class="border-box">

<div class="border-tl"><div class="border-tr"><div class="border-tc">
</div></div></div>
<div class="border-ml"><div class="border-mr">
<div class="border-mc float-break">
```

```
<h1>{$node.name|wash}</h1>
{include uri="design:parts/issue/entrymeta.tpl" node=$node}
<div class="entrybody">
    {attribute_view_gui attribute=$node.data_map.cover
                        alignment=left
                        image_class=medium
                        css_class=profile}
    {attribute_view_gui attribute=$node.data_map.short_description}
    {attribute_view_gui attribute=$node.data_map.description}
</div>
{include uri="design:parts/issue/authors.tpl" node=$node}
</div></div></div>
<div class="border-bl"><div class="border-br"><div class="border-bc">
</div></div></div>
    </div>
</div>
{if is_set($folder.0)}
<div class="articles">
    <div class="border-box">
<div class="border-tl"><div class="border-tr"><div class="border-tc">
</div></div></div>
<div class="border-ml"><div class="border-mr">
<div class="border-mc float-break">

<h1>{$folder.0.name}</h1>
{foreach $folder.0.children as $child}
    {node_view_gui content_node=$child.object.main_node
                view=line size="original"}
{/foreach}

</div></div></div>
<div class="border-bl"><div class="border-br"><div class="border-bc">
</div></div></div>
    </div>
</div>
{/if}
<div class="articles-list">
    <div class="border-box">

<div class="border-tl"><div class="border-tr"><div class="border-tc">
</div></div></div>
<div class="border-ml"><div class="border-mr">
<div class="border-mc float-break">

<h1>{"All articles"|i18n('design/magazine')}</h1>
{foreach $node.children as $child}
    {node_view_gui content_node=$child view=line}
{/foreach}
```

```
</div></div></div>
<div class="border-bl"><div class="border-br"><div class="border-bc">
</div></div></div>
   </div>
</div>
</div></div>

{undef $folder}
```

In this template, we have used a lot of functions and operators that we saw previously. There are only two interesting parts that we'll describe here.

The purpose of this template is to render the issue object with its cover and description in the leftmost column, the highlighted articles list in the rightmost column, and a list of all of the articles inside the issue in the bottom box.

The imported articles will be saved inside a folder in the issue object. To get the articles list, we have to use the following code:

```
{def $folder = fetch(content, list,
              hash('parent_node_id', $node.node_id,
                   'limit', 1,
                   'class_filter_type', 'include',
                   'class_filter_array', array('folder')))}
```

The function `list` of the module content returns an array. Inside it, we can find the children elements of the node identified by the `parent_node_id` parameter.

In this case, we will use a parameter of `limit` with a value equal to `1` because we want to use only the first element of the returned array — the `issue` folder.

As with the previous template, we again have to include two more subtemplates:

```
{include uri="design:parts/issue/entrymeta.tpl" node=$node}
{include uri="design:parts/issue/authors.tpl" node=$node}
```

The first subtemplate will display some information about the article, such as the publication date or the number of articles published in the issue.

```
<div class="entrymeta">{"Published on"|i18n('design/magazine')}
{$node.object.published|l10n( 'date' )} - {$node.children_count}
{"articles"|i18n('design/magazine')}</div>
```

The second subtemplate is the same as we used in the previous template. We will obtain this result:

Thumb template

This template will be used to show only the name and the cover of the issue object.

To edit this template, we need to open the `extension/packtmedia/design/magazine/override/templates/thumb/folder_issue.tpl` file, and add the following code to it:

```
<div class="content-view-thumb">
    <h2><a href={$node.url_alias|ezurl}>{$node.name}</a></h2>
    {attribute_view_gui attribute=$node.data_map.cover
                    image_class=small
                    href=$node.url_alias|ezurl(no)}
</div>
```

After we save it, the following page will be rendered:

Embed template

We will use this template to see the name of the issue. To modify it, we need to open the `extension/packtmedia/design/magazine/override/templates/embed/folder_issue.tpl` file, and add the following code to it:

```
<div class="content-view-full">
    <div class="class-folder">
        {$node.name|wash}
    </div>
</div>
```

Issue archive template

Next, we will look at all of the views for the folder that represents our "Issue archive".

Full template

We need to open the `extension/packtmedia/design/magazine/override/templates/full/folder_issuearchive.tpl` file, and add the following code to it:

```
{def $latest_issue_article = fetch(content, list,
                              hash('parent_node_id', $node.node_id,
                               'depth', 3,
                               'limit', 1,
                               'class_filter_type', 'include',
                               'class_filter_array', array('article'),
                              'sort_by', array( 'published', false() )))
   $latest_year = $node.children.0}
<div class="content-view-full">
   <div class="folder-issuearhive-full">

<div class="info">
   <div class="border-box">

<div class="border-tl"><div class="border-tr"><div class="border-tc">
</div></div></div>
<div class="border-ml"><div class="border-mr">
<div class="border-mc float-break">

<h1>{"Latest issue"|i18n('design/magazine')}</h1>
{node_view_gui content_node=$latest_issue_article.0.parent view=line}

</div></div></div>
<div class="border-bl"><div class="border-br"><div class="border-bc">
</div></div></div>

   </div>
</div>

<div class="articles">
   <div class="border-box">

<div class="border-tl"><div class="border-tr"><div class="border-tc">
</div></div></div>
<div class="border-ml"><div class="border-mr">
<div class="border-mc float-break">

<h1>{"%year% Issues"|i18n('design/magazine', '',
                   hash('%year%', $latest_year.name))}</h1>

{foreach $latest_year.children as $index => $child}
   {if $index|mod(3)|eq(0)}<div class="break"></div>{/if}
   {node_view_gui content_node=$child view=thumb}
{/foreach}

</div></div></div>
<div class="border-bl"><div class="border-br"><div class="border-bc">
</div></div></div>
```

```
        </div>
    </div>

    <div class="articles-list">
        <div class="border-box">

    <div class="border-tl"><div class="border-tr"><div class="border-tc">
    </div></div></div>
    <div class="border-ml"><div class="border-mr">
    <div class="border-mc float-break">

    <h2>{"Archive"|i18n('design/magazine')}</h1>

    {foreach $node.children as $year}
        <h2>{$year.name}</h2>
        <p>
        {foreach $year.children as $issue}
            <strong>{node_view_gui content_node=$issue view=text_linked}
            </strong>
            {delimiter}/{/delimiter}
        {/foreach}
        </p>
    {/foreach}

    </div></div></div>
    <div class="border-bl"><div class="border-br"><div class="border-bc">
    </div></div></div>

    </div></div>
    </div></div>
```

In this template, other than the structure that we already learned earlier in this chapter, we also use the mod operator. This returns the module of the two given parameters. In our case, it will print a `<div class="break"></div>` tag every time `$index` is a multiple of three. Moreover, we can see a more advanced use of the i18n operator through the strings parameterization. All of the parameters will be passed as a third parameter, by using an associative array. We will obtain this layout:

Embed template

This template will be used to render the name of the issue archive. We need to edit the `extension/packtmedia/design/magazine/override/templates/embed/folder_issuearchive.tpl` file, and add the following code to it:

```
<div class="content-view-full">
    <div class="class-folder">
        {$node.name|wash}
    </div>
</div>
```

Issue year template

Now, we have to create the "issue year" views. This will be a folder that will contain all of our past issues.

Full template

To edit the template, we need to open the `extension/packtmedia/design/`
`magazine/override/templates/full/folder_issueyear.tpl` file, and add the
following code to it:

```
<div class="content-view-full">
   <div class="folder-issuearhive-full">

<div class="info">
   <div class="border-box">

<div class="border-tl"><div class="border-tr"><div class="border-tc">
</div></div></div>
<div class="border-ml"><div class="border-mr">
<div class="border-mc float-break">

<h1>{"Latest issue"|i18n('design/magazine')}</h1>
{node_view_gui content_node=$node.children.0 view=line}

</div></div></div>
<div class="border-bl"><div class="border-br"><div class="border-bc">
</div></div></div>
   </div>
</div>

<div class="articles">
   <div class="border-box">

<div class="border-tl"><div class="border-tr"><div class="border-tc">
</div></div></div>
<div class="border-ml"><div class="border-mr">
<div class="border-mc float-break">

<h1>{"%year% Issues"|i18n('design/magazine', '', hash('%year%', $node.
name))}</h1>
{foreach $node.children as $index => $child}
   {if $index|mod(3)|eq(0)}<div class="break"></div>{/if}
   {node_view_gui content_node=$child.object.main_node view=thumb}
{/foreach}

</div></div></div>
<div class="border-bl"><div class="border-br">
<div class="border-bc"></div></div></div>

</div></div>
</div></div>
```

In this case, we will not introduce any new functions. However, we will use all the things that we learned before. The result will be as follows:

Issue article template

Next, we will look at the views for the class object article that represents the articles published inside an issue.

Line template

We need to modify the `extension/packtmedia/design/magazine/override/templates/line/issue_article.tpl` file, and add the following code to it:

```
<div class="content-view-line">
    <div class="article-line">
        <h2><a href={$node.url_alias|ezurl}>{$node.name}</a></h2>
        <div class="entrymeta">
```

```
            {"Published on"|i18n('design/magazine')}
            {$node.object.published|l10n( 'date' )}
        </div>
        {attribute_view_gui attribute=$node.data_map.intro}
        <div class="entrymeta">
            {"Written by"}
            {attribute_view_gui attribute=$node.data_map.author_profile}
        </div>
    </div>
</div>
```

Here, we will introduce the l10n operator, which gets an Epoch timestamp as input and returns a preformatted date that uses the correct internationalization for the language of the user.

This is what we will see:

Full template

For the template that will represent the articles, we will use the standard eZ Webin template file. We will edit some parts of it to better fit our needs.

We need to change the `extension/packtmedia/design/magazine/override/templates/full/issue_article.tpl` file, and add the following code to it:

```
<div class="border-box" style="float:left; width: 21%;margin-right:
    10px;">
<div class="border-tl"><div class="border-tr"><div class="border-tc">
</div></div></div>
<div class="border-ml"><div class="border-mr">
<div class="border-mc float-break">

<div class="cover">
    {node_view_gui content_node=$node.parent view=thumb}
    <h2>{"Related Articles"|i18n('design/magazine')}</h2>
    <ul style="margin: 0px;">
    {foreach $node.parent.children as $child}
    <li>{node_view_gui content_node=$child view=text_linked}</li>
{/foreach}
</ul>
</div>
</div></div></div>
<div class="border-bl"><div class="border-br"><div class="border-bc">
</div></div></div>
</div>
<div class="border-box" style="float: left; width: 77%;">
<div class="border-tl"><div class="border-tr"><div class="border-tc">
</div></div></div>
<div class="border-ml"><div class="border-mr">
<div class="border-mc float-break">

<div class="content-view-full">
    <div class="class-article">
    <h1>{$node.data_map.title.content|wash()}</h1>
    <div class="entrymeta">
    {"Published on"|i18n('design/magazine')}
    {$node.object.published|l10n( 'date' )}
    {"on"|i18n("design/magazine")} <a href=
        {$node.parent.url_alias|ezurl}>{$node.parent.name}</a></div>
{if eq( ezini( 'article', 'ImageInFullView', 'content.ini' ),
    'enabled' )}
    {if $node.data_map.image.has_content}
    <div class="attribute-image">
```

```
         {attribute_view_gui attribute=$node.data_map.image
                             image_class=medium}
         {if $node.data_map.caption.has_content}
         <div class="caption">
            {attribute_view_gui attribute=$node.data_map.caption}
         </div>
         {/if}
      </div>
      {/if}
   {/if}
   {if eq( ezini( 'article', 'SummaryInFullView', 'content.ini' ),
         'enabled' )}
      {if $node.data_map.intro.content.is_empty|not}
         <div class="attribute-short">
            {attribute_view_gui attribute=$node.data_map.intro}
         </div>
      {/if}
   {/if}
   {if $node.data_map.body.content.is_empty|not}
      <div class="attribute-long">
         {attribute_view_gui attribute=$node.data_map.body}
      </div>
   {/if}
      <div class="entrymeta">{"Written by"} {attribute_view_gui
         attribute=$node.data_map.author_profile}</div>
   {if is_unset( $versionview_mode )}
      {if $node.data_map.enable_comments.data_int}
         <h1>{"Comments"|i18n("design/ezwebin/full/article")}</h1>
         <div class="content-view-children">
         {foreach fetch_alias( comments, hash( parent_node_id,
            $node.node_id ) ) as $comment}
            {node_view_gui view='line' content_node=$comment}
         {/foreach}
         </div>
      {if fetch( 'content', 'access', hash( 'access', 'create',
                                    'contentobject', $node,
                                    'contentclass_id', 'comment' ) )}
      <form method="post" action={"content/action"|ezurl}>
      <input type="hidden" name="ClassIdentifier" value="comment" />
      <input type="hidden" name="NodeID"
            value="{$node.object.main_node.node_id}" />
      <input type="hidden" name="ContentLanguageCode"
            value="{ezini( 'RegionalSettings', 'Locale', 'site.ini')}" />
```

```
    <input class="button new_comment" type="submit" name="NewButton"
      value="{'New comment'|i18n( 'design/ezwebin/full/article' )}" />
</form>
    {else}
<p>{'%login_link_startLog in%login_link_end or %create_link_
startcreate a user account%create_link_end to comment.'|i18n( 'design/
ezwebin/full/article', , hash( '%login_link_start', concat( '<a
href="', '/user/login'|ezurl(no), '">' ), '%login_link_end', '</a>',
'%create_link_start', concat( '<a href="', "/user/register"|ezurl(no),
'">' ), '%create_link_end', '</a>' ) )}</p>
        {/if}
    {/if}
{/if}
{def $tipafriend_access=fetch( 'user', 'has_access_to',
    hash( 'module', 'content', 'function', 'tipafriend' ) )}
{if and( ezmodule( 'content/tipafriend' ), $tipafriend_access )}
    <div class="attribute-tipafriend">
        <p><a href={concat( "/content/tipafriend/", $node.node_id
)|ezurl} title="{'Tip a friend'|i18n( 'design/ezwebin/full/article'
)}">{'Tip a friend'|i18n( 'design/ezwebin/full/article' )}</a></p>
    </div>
{/if}
</div></div>
</div></div></div>
<div class="border-bl"><div class="border-br"><div class="border-bc">
</div></div></div>
</div>
```

We have added the leftmost block, which contains the cover issue and the related articles, by using the following code:

```
<div class="cover">
    {node_view_gui content_node=$node.parent view=thumb}
    <h2>{"Related Articles"|i18n('design/magazine')}</h2>
    <ul style="margin: 0px;">
    {foreach $node.parent.children as $child}
    <li>{node_view_gui content_node=$child view=text_linked}</li>
{/foreach}
</ul>
</div>
```

As the "issue" is the article parent, we used the attribute $node.parent to render the issue thumb. To print the list of the related articles, we created an unordered list containing all of the children of the parent node.

Additionally, we used the `ezini` operator to optionally print the data. The `ezini` operator reads and executes the directive written inside the `.ini` setting file.

This operator accepts three parameters:

1. The function name.
2. The parameter name for that function.
3. The name of the `.ini` file to read.

As an example, in the code, we have:

```
{if eq( ezini( 'article', 'SummaryInFullView', 'content.ini' ),
      'enabled' )}
```

This will read the `SummaryInFullView` parameter from the section `article` of the `content.ini` file and all it appends. If the `ezini` return is `enabled`, the `if` statement will be executed.

The last two code blocks are used to display the comments and the `tipafriend` functionality.

The comment block needs some further discussion.

```
{if is_unset( $versionview_mode )}
    {if $node.data_map.enable_comments.data_int}
        <h1>{"Comments"|i18n("design/ezwebin/full/article")}</h1>
        <div class="content-view-children">
        {foreach fetch_alias( comments, hash( parent_node_id,
                               $node.node_id ) ) as $comment}
            {node_view_gui view='line' content_node=$comment}
        {/foreach}
        </div>
    {if fetch( 'content', 'access', hash( 'access', 'create',
                              'contentobject', $node,
                              'contentclass_id', 'comment' ) )}
    <form method="post" action={"content/action"|ezurl}>
    <input type="hidden" name="ClassIdentifier" value="comment" />
    <input type="hidden" name="NodeID"
           value="{$node.object.main_node.node_id}" />
    <input type="hidden" name="ContentLanguageCode"
        value="{ezini( 'RegionalSettings', 'Locale', 'site.ini')}" />
    <input class="button new_comment" type="submit" name="NewButton"
      value="{'New comment'|i18n( 'design/ezwebin/full/article' )}" />
    </form>
    {else}
```

```
<p>{'%login_link_startLog in%login_link_end or %create_link_
startcreate a user account%create_link_end to comment.'|i18n( 'design/
ezwebin/full/article', , hash( '%login_link_start', concat( '<a
href="', '/user/login'|ezurl(no), '">' ), '%login_link_end', '</a>',
'%create_link_start', concat( '<a href="', "/user/register"|ezurl(no),
'">' ), '%create_link_end', '</a>' ) )}</p>
    {/if}
{/if}
{/if}
```

All of this code is used only if the `$versionview_mode` variable is not set. This is used only in the preview mode.

If the `$versionview_mode` variable is not used and the `$node.data_map.enable_comments.data_int` attribute is equal to 1, all of the comment children of the article node can be retrieved through the `fetch_alias` function:

```
fetch_alias( comments, hash( parent_node_id, $node.node_id ) )
```

This function allows the creation of a fetch function alias in order to permit the use of same function more than one time within the same template. To create a fetch function, we have to override the `fetchalias.ini` file.

As we print the comments list, we want to display a button to add a new comment if the user has the correct permission.

To do that, we have to add the following code:

```
{if fetch( 'content', 'access', hash( 'access', 'create',
                                'contentobject', $node,
                                'contentclass_id', 'comment' ) )}
<form method="post" action={"content/action"|ezurl}>
<input type="hidden" name="ClassIdentifier" value="comment" />
<input type="hidden" name="NodeID"
       value="{$node.object.main_node.node_id}" />
<input type="hidden" name="ContentLanguageCode"
       value="{ezini( 'RegionalSettings', 'Locale', 'site.ini')}" />
<input class="button new_comment" type="submit" name="NewButton"
    value="{'New comment'|i18n( 'design/ezwebin/full/article' )}" />
</form>
```

The fetch access function of the content module is the one that checks whether the user has the appropriate credentials perform a given action. We use it to check whether the user has permission to create a new object of the comment class inside the selected node.

The following form is used to generate the creation page of a new object in eZ Publish.

If the user doesn't have the required permission, the following code will be rendered by the system to show the login and sign in links:

```
{else}
<p>{'%login_link_startLog in%login_link_end or %create_link_
startcreate a user account%create_link_end to comment.'|i18n( 'design/
ezwebin/full/article', , hash( '%login_link_start', concat( '<a
href="', '/user/login'|ezurl(no), '">' ), '%login_link_end', '</a>',
'%create_link_start', concat( '<a href="', "/user/register"|ezurl(no),
'">' ), '%create_link_end', '</a>' ) )}</p>
    {/if}
```

In this code, we use the i18n function, parameterized as we saw before.

The last code block is used by the tipafriend functionality. To use it, we don't need to do anything because it is embedded inside of eZ Publish by default, and allows the current page link to be sent to a predefined email address.

The required code is:

```
{def $tipafriend_access=fetch( 'user', 'has_access_to',
                       hash( 'module', 'content',
                             'function', 'tipafriend' ) )}

{if and( ezmodule( 'content/tipafriend' ), $tipafriend_access )}
    <div class="attribute-tipafriend">
        <p><a href={concat( "/content/tipafriend/", $node.node_id
) |ezurl} title="{'Tip a friend'|i18n( 'design/ezwebin/full/article'
)}">{'Tip a friend'|i18n( 'design/ezwebin/full/article' )}</a></p>
    </div>
{/if}
```

This code introduces the has_access_to fetch function of the user module, which checks whether the user can use the tipafriend function of the content module.

The page will be rendered as shown here:

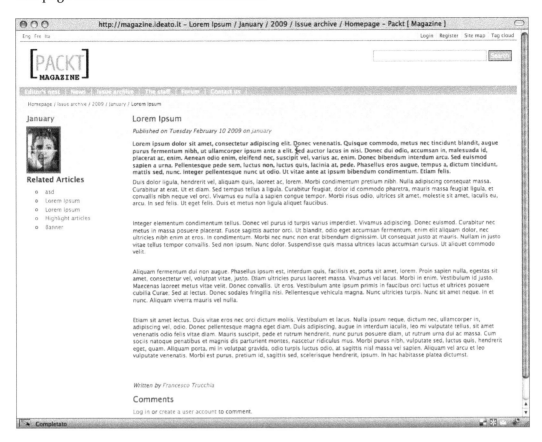

Embed template

This template will be used to render the issue article title. To use it, we have to edit the `extension/packtmedia/design/magazine/override/templates/embed/issue_article.tpl` file, and add the following code to it:

```
<div class="content-view-full">
    <div class="class-article">
        {$node.name|wash}
    </div>
</div>
```

Summary

In this chapter, we learned how to create override rules for our classes, in both automatic mode and manual mode. Moreover, we saw how to create a custom template based on these override rules. We also saw in detail all of the custom templates for our project. In the next chapter, we will learn how to use the forum and blog functionality of the eZ Webin package.

8

Adding Community Forums

The open society, the unrestricted access to knowledge, the unplanned and uninhibited association of men for its furtherance — these are what may make a vast, complex, ever growing, ever changing, ever more specialized and expert technological world, nevertheless a world of human community.

— J Robert Oppenheimer

In the previous chapter, we created our entire layout structure. Now, we will use this layout structure, without additional enhancements, to fully host the magazine's forum.

In this chapter, we will:

- Take a look at the built-in forums available through the eZ Webin packages
- Use and configure the content classes and functionality to create a community system for our magazine
- Learn how the eZ Webin blog content class works
- Create an editor blog

The magazine's forum

As we learned in the previous chapters, eZ Webin comes bundled with a lot of useful features and extensions. One of these is the **forum** data object, which allows us to create a complete community bulletin board application without writing a single line of code.

Adding the Forum

To add a forum, we have to log in to the eZ Webin backend from `http://packtmediaproject/index.php/ezwebin_site_admin/`. From the **Content structure** tab, we have to add a new **Forums** object by using the drop-down menu located at the bottom of the page as shown here:

Next, we have to set up the name of the forum and add a simple description, in order to better describe it:

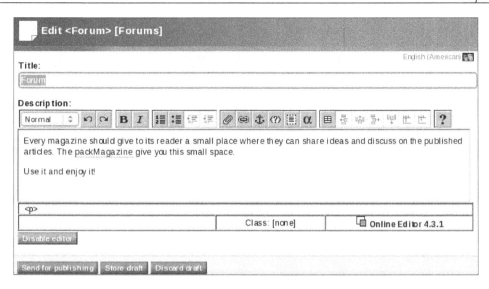

After we save the **Forums** object, we can start to populate it by using the **Forum** objects. The difference between the two dataobjects is that the former acts as a container or repository for the forum structure, whereas the latter is a container for the **Forum topic** dataobject.

As before, we can add a **Forum** object by using the drop-down menu at the bottom of the page, as shown here:

We can create a lot of different forums on our site—one for every argument that we want to talk about.

In the screenshot, we can see some of the topics that we created for the site's forum. We created a **Chitchat** forum for non-technical related issues, a **Tech and gadgets** forum where users can discuss new technologies, a **Programming stuff** forum related to web development, and a **Church of Emacs Vs Cult of VI** forum for software comparison discussions.

Creating a sticky post

It is useful to add a sticky post to give the required importance to a particular argument, which is also referred to as **thread**. For example, the forum rules should always be visible at the top of the selected forum.

To create a sticky post, we have to add a **Forum topic** to the Forum object, by using the drop-down bar that we used before, and select the checkbox named **Sticky**.

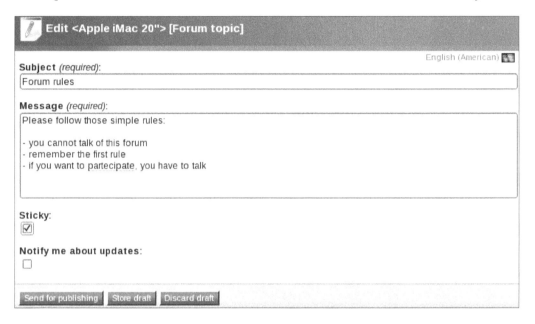

Forum access control list

The bulletin board provided by eZ Publish is not as powerful as some renowned ones, such as vBulletin or phpBB, but it has all of the basic features required of a multipurpose CMF in order to manage a simple forum. Moreover, the eZ Publish forum object is released with some default configuration that is useful for instantiating it and using it immediately. For example, the default access control list of the forum object is set to allow to an anonymous user to read the forums and all of the threads, but to only allow registered users to write on it.

If we want to change the permissions for a single Forum channel—for example, by creating a private forum that only certain users can see—we have to use the **Roles and policies** functionality provided by the CMF.

We saw this menu in the previous chapters, when we created a new section for our site. Now, we will use it to create a private forum only for the users in the **Editor role** group.

Creating the Private forums section

First of all, we need to create a new **Section** called **Private forums**. To do this, we will open the **Setup** tab in the backend, and then click on the **Sections** link in the leftmost sidebar. As we did before, we will create a new section by clicking on the **New section** button.

We will call the new section **Private forums**. Next, we will select **Content structure** from the **Navigation part** drop-down list.

Next, we will click on the **OK** button, after which we will be redirected to the section's list page. Here, we need to click on the plus icon (+), which is displayed on the rightmost side of the screen, to assign the selected section to a content subtree.

Navigate to the selected forum(s) that you want to assign as private, and select the appropriate checkbox. Then, to save your selection, click on the **Select** button.

Now, the forum will be inaccessible to all users except those in the Administration role group.

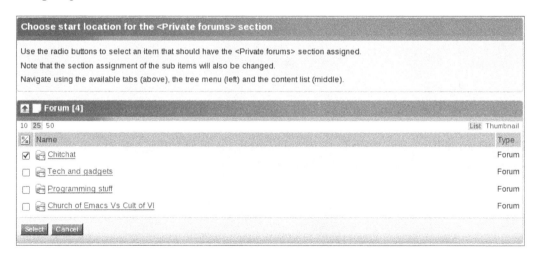

We have to grant users who are editors the ability to see the private forum. After we open the **Roles and policies** link in the **Setup** tab, we have to click on the **Editor** link.

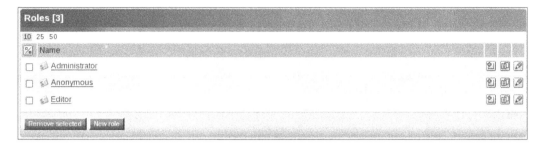

Here, we will select the **Subtree** option from the drop-down menu located at the bottom of the **Users and groups using the <Editor> role** box, and then click on the **Assign with limitation** button.

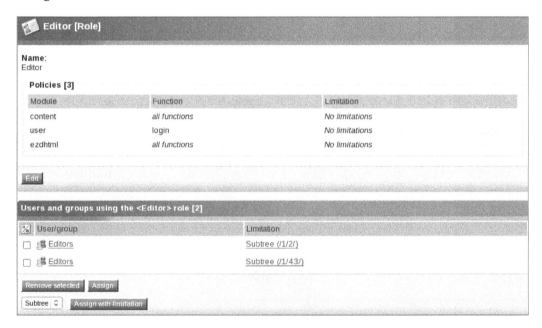

The system will ask us which section we want to enable for this role group. We will choose the **Private forums** section that we created previously.

Next, we need to confirm the users (or the user groups) to be assigned to the section. We will again choose the **Editors**. Save your work by clicking on the **Select** button. Now, all of the users that we created in this group should be able to see and use the private forums.

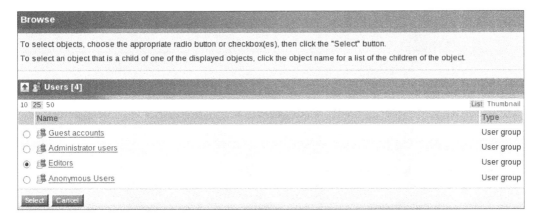

Creating the magazine's blog

As for the forum, we need some service for our site to give it a *Web 2.0 dimension*. The real killer application is the blog. Here, the editors should be able to freely write about their views and company news, and provide a *human face* to a company-related site.

Installing a blog application is very easy, and the eZ Webin package comes in handy again for doing this. This package gives us features such as the tagging and comment systems, and the post calendar widget.

Adding the blog

The blog engine relies on two content classes: **blog** and **blog post**. The first one acts as a container for the post, whereas the second is used to write new posts.

To add a blog to our site, we have to go to the backend and add a blog object as a child of the home page.

Next, we have to specify the name of the blog—in our case **Editor's nest**—and then provide a description of the blog:

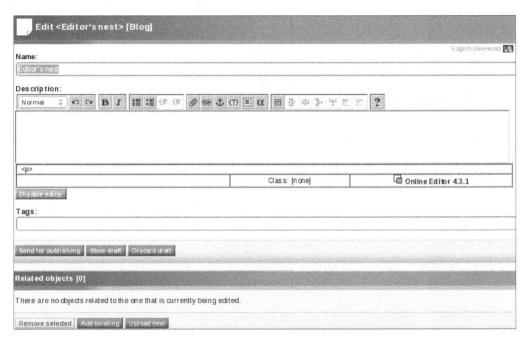

After we add this class, the blog will appear on the relative path in the public siteaccess with the default templating of the eZ Webin package. We can see this in the next screenshot.

Changing the blog layout

We can change the layout of the blog (for example, to remove the calendar) at any moment. We simply have to overwrite the eZ Webin blog template located in the `packtmediaproject/extension/ezwebin/design/ezwebin/templates/parts/blog` folder with the one that we will create in our extension, as we did in the Chapter 7, for the default eZ Webin template.

Set up the feeds

A **feed** (or **news feed**) is a data format used for providing users with frequently-updated content, such as news for a site, or posts for a blog. A feed can be provided in different formats, such as RSS or ATOM, and can be subscribed by a user with a feed reader application.

Adding feeds to a site is very important because it provides users with the latest content without them having to visit the site.

By default, eZ Publish doesn't provide a self-generated feed. However, it does provide an option for the site administrator to enable one from the administration interface.

Moreover, any node of the content tree can be used to generate a feed, through a very flexible system that can handle any kind of content class.

We will add a feed to the forums and the blog, choosing the best class attributes for both.

Creating the blog feed

Log in to the backend. From the **Setup** tab, we will click on the **RSS** link in the left-hand sidebar.

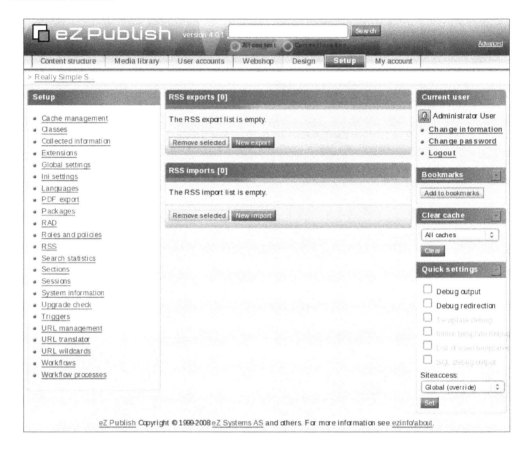

Next, click on the **New Export** button and complete the form with the necessary data for our new feed, which is a **Name**, a **Description**, and a **Site URL**.

In this form, eZ Publish will require some information regarding the feed itself, as we can see in the following screenshots:

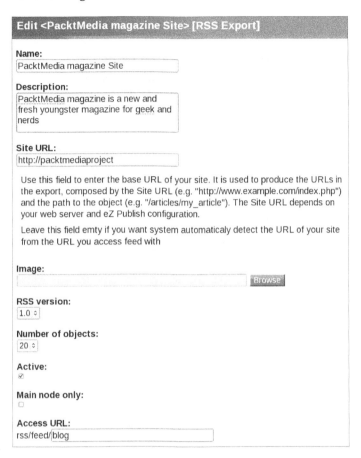

The feed information includes the following:

- **Name**: The name of the feed that we will publish.

- **Description**: The text used to describe the feed.

- **Site URL**: This is used to produce URLs in the export, comprised of the Site URL (`http://www.packtmediamagazine.com/index.php`) and the path to the object (`/articles/my_article`). Leave this field empty if you want the system to automatically detect the URL of your site from the URL that you access the feed with.

- **Image**: This image will be attached to the feed, as a favicon.

- **RSS version**: This is the version of the RSS format that is used by eZ Publish in order to publish the feed.

- **Number of objects**: This value represents the number of objects that we want to add to the feed.

- **Active**: This checkbox will be used to enable or disable the feed.

- **Main node only**: If checked, only the main node will be selected otherwise the children node will be added to the feed.

- **Access URL**: This represents the feed URL. By default, eZ Publish uses the reserved prefix path **/rss/feed/**. We have to create a valid **Access URL** as **blog**.

After we define the feed's information, we have to configure the sources from where we want to retrieve the objects to be taken for the feed. We can do this by completing the **Source 1** subform as shown:

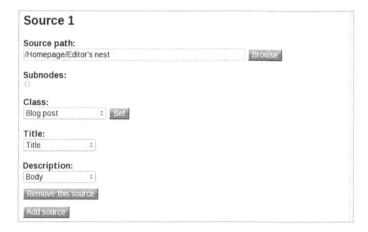

To configure the feed source, we have to define:

- **Source path**: This is the path of the navigation tree of the site from which we want to gather the data.

- **Subnodes**: If enabled, the subnodes of the main node will also be used.

- **Class**: We can filter the object class that we want to add to the feed. In our case, we will choose the **Blog post** class.

- **Title**: We can choose which attribute of the **Blog post** class we want to use as the title of the single feed.

- **Description**: In this field, we can choose which attribute will be used as a description for the feed. In our case, it will be the **Body** attribute of the **Blog Post** class.

- **Remove/Add Source buttons**: These buttons will add or remove the settings that we have configured.

When we configure the **Source path,** by clicking on the **Browse** button, eZ Publish will ask us to choose the node that we want to use to create the feed.

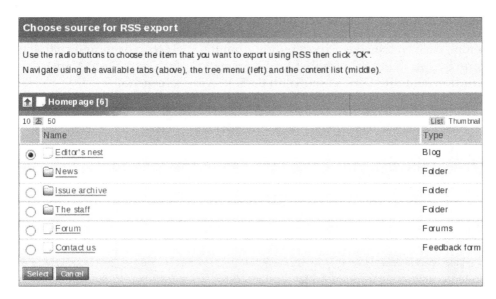

As shown in the previous screenshot, we will select the **blog** node as the primary source. This will ask the system to check for content only in that node, and to not use the whole site.

Next, we will choose which classes we want to include in the feed, and which class attributes should be used for the feed title and content.

For the blog, we will use the **Blog post** class. After we click on the **Set** button to refresh the class attributes, we will select the **Title** and **Body** attributes for the feed **Title** and **Description** respectively.

Next, click on the **OK** button to save your settings and check for the feed.

You can see if the feed is enabled by taking a look at the navigation toolbar in any modern browser. For example, in any 3.x version of Firefox, the feed icon will appear on the left-hand side of the domain name. This is seen in the following screenshot:

Creating the forum feed

We have an additional requirement for the forum. We want to include all of the new discussions in a single feed, which will create a kind of aggregate feed.

As before, click on the **New export** button from the RSS setup page, and complete the form by specifying the required feed information, such as the feed **Name**, **Description**, and **Site URL** as shown in the following screenshot:

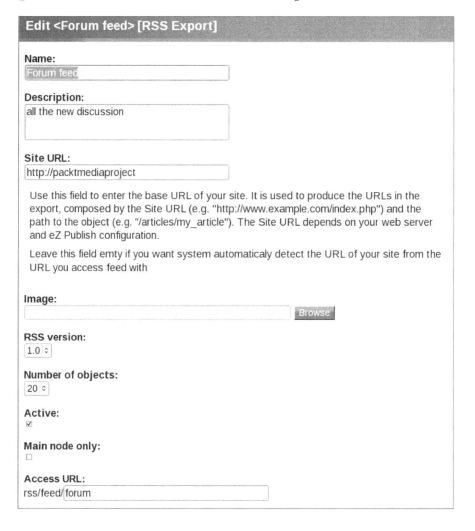

The main difference between this and the previous example is in the **Source 1** subform, where we will select the **/Homepage/Forum** as the **Source path,** and select the **Subnodes** checkbox. This is shown in the following screenshot:

This setting will cause a full parse of the selected node to be made, in order to check if any subnodes with the specified content class exist, and will then add any such subnodes to the feed.

Multi-source feed

eZ Publish allows us to create a multi-source feed. For example, if we create some blogs on different document tree nodes, we can include all of them in our feed by using the **Add source** button in the RSS edit page. In fact, clicking on that button will create a new sub-section called (in our case) **Source 2**, where we can configure a new **Source Path** that will be merged with the one that we configured before.

Summary

In this chapter, we discovered the social features provided by the eZ Webin package, and enabled these for our magazine site. Also, we learned how to create a feed for both a single type of content and for aggregated content. In the next chapter, we will see how internationalization and localization work in the CMF.

9
Internationalization and Localization

oct 31 = dec 25

A mathematical joke

In this chapter, we will provide a brief overview of:

- The internationalization capabilities of eZ Publish, and will implement some additional language translations for our customers who may be visiting and looking to enroll themselves in the magazine
- How to use the eZ Publish backend to translate articles and content classes, and then publish them

A multilingual site

Internationalization and localization are two big issues for people who need to develop a multilingual site. Other than the simple text translation, a developer needs to know how the local standard formats—such as dates, numbers, or amounts—change from country to country. Internationalization and localization take care of these problems.

Internationalization

Internationalization, often referred to as **i18n** (the number represents the count of the letters in the word), is the practice of creating software so that it isn't hard-wired to one language, locale, or culture.

For example, the workflow of a contact form will work in the same way even if the page contains English or Italian text.

Fortunately, eZ Publish allows the implementation of internationalization for any single object that it can manage. This will help us in translating language templates, content objects, attributes, and much more.

Localization

The localization process (**L10n**) helps site administrators to assign the correct values according to the country language displayed. This means that you not only show the translated text, but also dates in the appropriate format based on the languages used. For example, in the English interface, a date is based on the month/day/year format, whereas in the Italian interface, a date is represented in the day/month/year format.

To manage the country-specific settings, eZ Publish uses the **locale identifier**.

Locale identifiers

A locale identifier consists of a language code of three letters (**ita**), followed by two uppercase letters (**IT**) for the country code. This identifier is based on the **ISO 639** (`http://www.iso.org/iso/iso_catalogue/catalogue_tc/catalogue_detail.htm?csnumber=22109http://it.wikipedia.org/wiki/ISO_639`) and **ISO 3166-1** (`http://it.wikipedia.org/wiki/ISO_3166-1`) standards.

eZ Publish uses the default locale, the United Kingdom English language (**eng-GB**), and has a lot of pre-defined locale settings in the `.ini` file located in the `share/locale` directory of the installation root.

Creating a new locale file

eZ Publish has a lot of default locale settings. However, a specific behavior or language may not be provided. To create a new locale, we should copy one of the standard files provided in the `share/locale` folder and overwrite it with the necessary content. We can also send our job to the contributions page (`http://ez.no/developer/contribs/internationalization`) at the `ez.no` site. From the same site, we can also download a lot of updated locale files.

As an example, if we need to create a Klingonian locale file based on English language, we have to open a shell to create the new file in this way:

```
# cp share/locale/eng-GB.ini share/locale/kln-KL.ini
```

Next, we will edit the new `kln-KL.ini` file by adding the country's locale settings.

After we create the locale file, we also have to create a translation file for the eZ Publish main interface. We can find translation files in the `share/translations` directory, placed in the root of the system.

As we can see, this folder contains a set of subfolders named with the locale identifier (such as, `ita-IT`). These subfolders contain a `translation.ts` XML file that can be used to translate the localization strings from the default eZ Publish English to the locale language.

eZ Publish has, by default, an untranslated folder that can be used as a template for creating a new, clean translation file. To create our translation file for the new locale, we have to execute the following command from the eZ Publish installation path:

```
# cp -Rf share/translations/untraslated/ share/translations/kln-KL
```

Now, we can easily translate the file's entries by using software such as QtLinguist (`http://www.qtsoftware.com/products/developer-tools`).

 You can find more information on this software application in the QTLinguist manual on the QT technical documentation site: `http://doc.trolltech.com/4.5/linguist-manual.html`.

Anatomy of the translations.ts file

The `translations.ts` file is an XML file that contains information on how to translate a particular string.

The structure of the file is based on a `context` tag, which contains a unique identifier called `name`, a `message` tag with the original text `source`, and the relative `translation` file. As an example, the following is an extract from the eZ Webin `translation.ts` file:

```
<context>
    <name>design/ezwebin/article/article_index</name>
    <message>
        <source>Article index</source>
        <translation>Indice articolo</translation>
    </message>
</context>
```

Note that the `translations.ts` file should be encoded with UTF8 so that it can be opened with QtLinguist.

Multi-language site management

In Chapter 1, during the installation, we enabled the support for multi-language in eZ Publish. Then in Chapter 2, we created site accesses for those languages, by adding failover capabilities to the CMF if content is not translated in the main language. The next step is to manage the language from the eZ Webin backend.

Log in to the backend from `http://packtmediaproject/index.php/dev_panel/` and then, in the **Setup** tab, click on the **Languages** link in the leftmost menu.

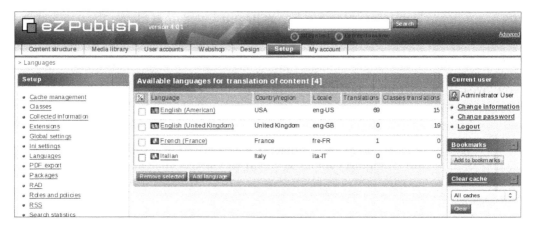

Here, we can see all of the enabled languages and the related translated objects. If we click on a language, eZ Publish will show all the locale info settings for that language.

From this page, we can also add to or remove new languages from the CMF easily, as we did from the shell.

We can remove a language only if it does not contain any content objects.

Class attribute translations

As noted earlier, eZ Publish allows translating any single object or attribute. This is very useful for displaying the attribute labels in the correct language in the backend or the frontend of the CMF.

To translate a class object, we need to go in the **Setup** tab and then click on the **Classes** links located in the leftmost menu.

Here, we can see a list of all of the content classes that have been created in the CMF. To translate them, we have to select them one by one, and then add the translation. As an example, we will translate the **Article** class.

After we click on the name of the class, we will be redirected to the class summary page.

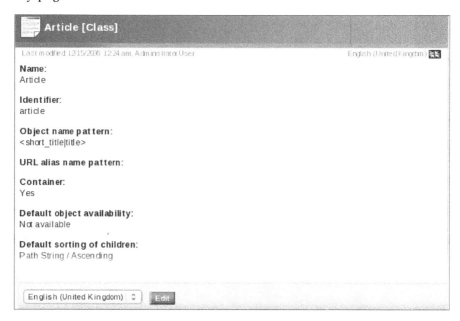

Here we can see all of the information related to the class and, moreover, we can edit it by adding new attributes or managing the languages. From the drop-down box, select the **Another language** link, and then click on the **Edit** button.

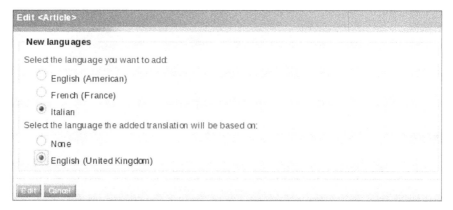

The system will ask us which language we want to enable for the class. We can select one of the installed languages, and also on which translated language we want to base the new translation. This should be very useful for languages such as **eng-GB** or **eng-US**, where only small cosmetic changes need to be made.

After we select the new language, we need to click on the **Edit** button, and can then start translating all of the contents of the page.

The edit form that opens is the same as the one that we saw in Chapter 3 when we created the content object for the articles. In this case, we don't need to add anything new except for the translated strings. For example, we start by translating the **Article** object into Italian, giving its Italian name **Articolo,** and the translation for the title value (**Titolo**).

Apart from the strings, we can also change the default behavior of the content attributes, adding — for example — a default value for the publication date (instead of an empty value), or removing a searchable flag.

After we have translated everything, and saved our work by clicking the **OK** button, we will be redirected to the class summary page for the newly inserted language.

Class default language

If our editors are from Italy, we can choose to use Italian as the default language for the entire content class.

To do this, in the **Classes** link of the **Setup** tab, locate the class that you wish to edit and click on the name of the class. Then, enable the translations window, select the desired language using the option buttons, and save your changes by using the **Set main** button. This is shown in the following screenshot:

Content translation

As for the content classes, we can translate any content object created in the CMF. To do this, we need to open the **Content structure** tab, and choose the object that needs to be translated.

We can now select which language we want to add to the document, and start working on it. After we publish our work by using the **Send for publishing** button, the new translation will be available on the site frontend, under the selected language.

URL translation

When we translate a content object, its main URL will change accordingly. But we should only need to create aliases for a single language. For example, we should create an alias for the contact page in the staff section of the site only for the Italian version.

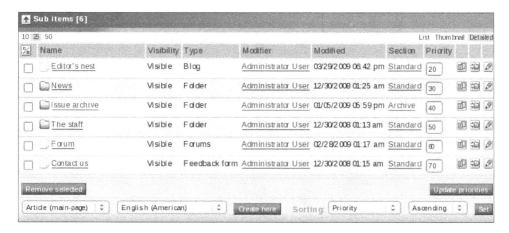

As the first step, we need to open the **Content structure** tab. Next, from the **Sub items** box of the home page, we need to click on the icon for the **Contact Us** content object.

The context menu will appear. Here, we have to select the **Advanced | Manage URL aliases** link.

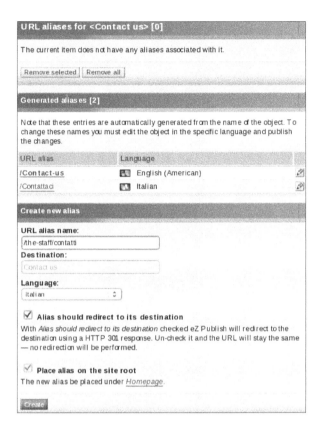

We can add a new URL alias by entering the new URL manually and selecting the relative language.

When we create a complex URL alias based on the pre-existing URL path, we have to remember that the existing objects or functionality with the same name will take precedence over the alias name.

Multilingual extensions

We saw how to create a new locale file and how to compile a translations file. Now we will see how to upgrade our extension to i18n.

The extension folder structure

To enable multilingual support in our extension, we have to create a new folder structure for the translation files. We have to open a shell, go to the extension folder, and then create a directory named `translations`.

```
# cd /var/www/packtmediaproject/extension/packtmedia
# mkdir translations
# mkdir translations/ita-IT
# mkdir translations/fra-FR
# mkdir translations/de-DE
```

For all of the folders, we have to create the `translation.ts` file named according to the string that we will use in the templates.

The extension siteaccess

As for the main siteaccess that we configured in Chapter 2, we have to notify the system to also enable the internationalization system for our extension. To do this, we need to open the `site.ini.append.php` file located in the extension `settings/` directory.

```
# cd /var/www/packtmediaproject/extension/packtmedia
# cd settings
# vi site.ini.append.php
```

Now, add the following lines to the bottom of the `site.ini.append.php` file:

```
[RegionalSettings]
TranslationExtensions[]=packtmedia
```

As we can see in the above code, the `TranslatedExtensions` array parameter is used to enable the internationalization system for the named extensions, in this case `packtmedia`.

After we configure the `RegionalSettings` section, we have to clear the eZ Publish cache to let the system know that the extension will use the internationalization features of the CMF, and to let the system know that it will have to search for the required translation files.

The template strings

One of the first things to do is to replace all of the hardcoded text that we placed in the templates files using the i18n and l10n operators.

These operators are quite easy to use; we saw them in Chapter 7 when we customized the override template for the profile pages.

```
{'Original string'|i18n( 'design/packmedia/content/newstring' )}
```

The i18n operator allows us to change the string placed before the pipe with the one identified by the unique name that we pass as the first parameter.

```
{$node.object.published|l10n( 'date' )}
```

Here, the l10n operator will help us to format miscellaneous numeric values according to the current locale settings as dates, times, currencies, numbers.

Summary

In this chapter, we learned how to manage internationalization and localization for both content and classes. We looked at how to create custom translation files for our extension, and we used the eZ Webin backend to publish the translated object. In the next chapter, we will talk about roles and privileges by going into what we learned in the previous chapters, in greater detail.

10
Creating Roles and Privileges

Do it! Do it!

Starsky & Hutch movie

After all of this defining and creating, we need to put some order in the house. In this chapter, we will create privileges and roles for the users that allow them to do only the required tasks. We will learn about the ACL system, how the permission system of eZ Publish works, and will create the groups and the roles needed by the site. Then, we will look at the workflow system and create a notification workflow for the site's blog.

Policies, roles, and groups

When we work in a big company, everyone has his or her own role, tasks, and permissions. For example, an advertising guy will never touch a server, and a web designer will not write a contract. eZ Publish is like a big company, where the administrator can do everything, or can delegate specific tasks to users or group of users. This behavior is called **ACL** (**Access Control List**) and is based on roles, policies, and groups.

Moreover, as in any big company, eZ Publish needs to verify that its employee is who he claims to be, and needs to allow him to read the content that he can access.

Luckily, eZ Pubish has these features natively integrated into its core, as user account management.

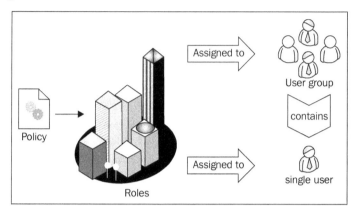

Policies

A policy is an atomic right that allows a user to use a given functionality of a module, for example, to create a new blog post in the blog. A policy is based on three parts: a module name, the name of one of the functions of the module, and a permission on that function. If we think about the previous example (creating a new blog post in the blog), the policies allow a user to access the create function of content modules of the **Blog post** class object.

We have to remember that we can create a policy to use all of the functions of a particular module and that not all of the functions need to be limited. Moreover, the limitations may change from module to module.

Roles

When we put a bunch of policies together, we create a role. We can assign a role to either a single user or to a group of users. A role can also be limited to a particular section or navigation sub-tree. Using the policies example again, we can assign the policy to create a blog post to a role, and then assign this role to two groups. However, whereas the first group will create a blog post everywhere, the other group will be limited to a particular section of the site.

Applying a role

We can use three main strategies to apply a role to a group (or a user) — all of them with their pros and cons.

The first strategy is to create many atomic roles, all of them with specific policies. This solution allows us to create and manage small roles. But we have to add, for example, both the Anonymous and Editor roles to the Editor groups to allow them to read public content.

The second solution use with a different approach. The roles will have all of the policies required to fulfill a particular task. For example, the Editor role will also include all of the policies of the Anonymous role. In this case, if we change the policies of the Anonymous role, not all of the groups that have Editor role will be involved.

The third solution is to create groups with a very small subset of roles, and then add all of them directly to the users. This solution is optimal for managing specific users, but it is not recommended for a site that has a lot of users and groups.

Obviously, we can also merge and combine the three approaches, but we suggest to always keep it as simple as possible.

User groups

As the name suggests, a **User group** is a collection of users. eZ Publish represents user groups as specific nodes that contain user accounts. A user group can also contain another user group.

When we talk about users, we have to remember that they are also eZ Publish content objects that contain particular information regarding the user itself, which is provided by the **User account** datatype.

As with the Folder content classes, which can contain other Folder objects or other kind of content objects, both User Groups and Users are managed by eZ Publish as content classes. This means that we can change and extend them at any time, in order to fulfill our needs.

eZ Publish user management

We saw how eZ Publish roles and policies work in Chapter 6, when we created a new section, and then in Chapter 8, when we added specific policies to a forum channel.

But we never talked about how the CMF manages users.

User accounts

Every time that we have to deal with a user, we will find the relative content object inside the **User accounts** tab.

On the left-hand sidebar of this section of eZ Publish, we can see the user groups that have been created. Also, we can see in the main content area all of the information for the area.

If we click on a user group on the left, the central area will be expanded to show an **Assigned roles** box.

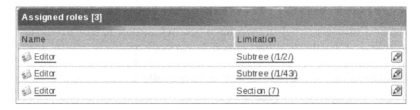

This contains all of the roles applied to the group, and specifies if there are any section or subtree limitations.

Within this box, we can find the **Available policies** box, as shown here:

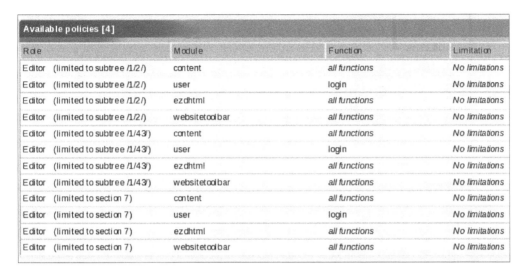

This box is a drill-down of the first one, and all of the relative policies of the applied roles are shown in it.

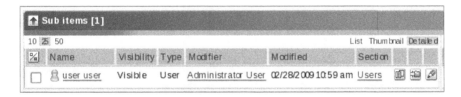

The last box, called **Sub items**, is the container of all of the users that belong to the group.

As for the other content object, a user can be disabled by adding an 'invisible' tag, and edited, directly from here.

Creating a new user

eZ Webin allows us to create users in two ways: via the predefined registration form in the frontend, or from the administration backend.

The following screenshot shows how the registration form on the frontpage of the site appears, using the predefined eZ Webin template with our CSS:

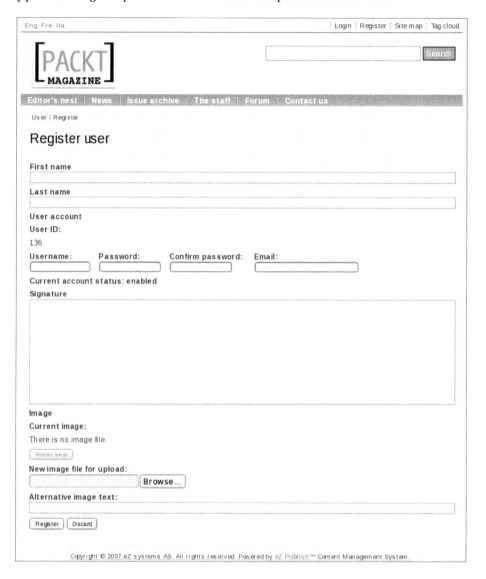

When the users register themselves via the frontend, they will be saved as **Anonymous Users** and the default roles will be applied.

Otherwise, in order to create a new user from the backend, we have to log in from the backend interface located at `http://packtmediaproject/index.php/dev_panel`. Now, from the **User accounts** tab, we have to open the group into which we want to place the new user.

Here, we can use the drop-down menu at the bottom of the content area to create a new **User** or a **User group** content object.

The following screenshot shows the backend interface used to create a new user:

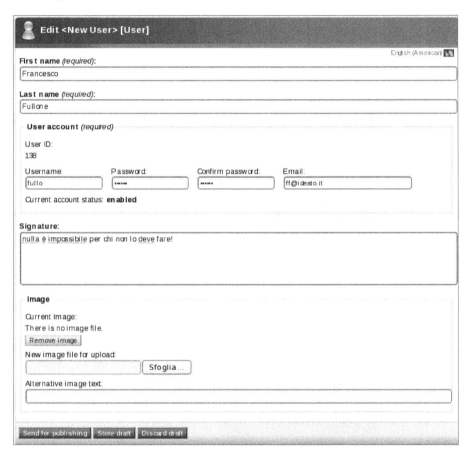

When we create a new user via the backend, we have to provide the same data as we do when creating a user via the frontend. The only difference is that, in this case, we can create the user in the exact group that we want.

 It's very important to remember that eZ Publish checks for a unique username and email address. So two different users cannot have this information duplicated.

Extending eZ Publish user classes

When we created the new user, we noticed that we can create only Users or User groups; but we defined our profile content class to manage the editors in Chapter 3. To add this content class to the **User accounts** content area, we will need to update it.

Open the **Setup** tab, and then click on the **Classes** link in the sidebar. Then, click on the **Content** class inside the **Class group** box, and select the **Profile** content class, in order to see its information. At the bottom of the page, we can see the **Member of class groups** box, as seen in the following screenshot:

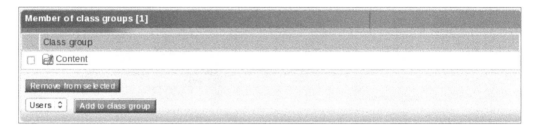

In this box, select **Users** from the drop-down menu, and then click on the **Add to class group** button. From now on, we'll be able to create new profile editors inside the Editors user group.

Managing a user

Sometimes we may need to delete a user, for example, an employee who leaves our company, or an external user who wants to delete his own profile.

In this case, we can proceed in two ways. We can either delete the user permanently, or disable the user by maintaining the author's attributes on the content that he or she created.

Disabling a user

To disable a user, we have to open the **User accounts** tab in the backend, and then browse in the categories for the user that we want to disable.

Open the user page, and in the **Preview** page, click on the **Configure user account settings** link. The following window will be displayed:

Deselect the **Enable user account** checkbox, and save your changes by clicking on the **OK** button.

Deleting a user

To delete a user, we have to select the user from the **User group** page, and select the relevant checkbox.

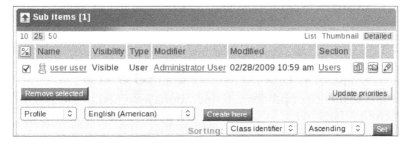

Next, when we will click on the **Remove selected** button, the system will ask us how to proceed.

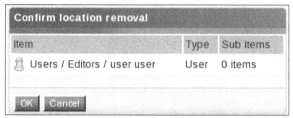

Click on the **OK** button and the user has now been deleted.

The eZ Webin predefined groups

As we saw when we created the new interface and content classes, the eZ Webin packages come with a handful of preconfigured features.

In this case, the package automatically creates five different groups, along with the relevant roles and privileges.

We can see these groups in the following table:

Administrator users	The users who belong to this group are superusers, having access to all of the functionality of eZ Publish.
Editors	These users can manage the content of the CMF.
Partners	These are member users with the privileges necessary to use a reserved area of the frontend.
Members	These are anonymous users who have registered themselves. These members can manage their personal profile page.
Anonymous users	Visitors who are not logged in. They can read everything that is marked as public.

 For all of the users, irrespective of whether they are logged in or not, eZ Publish will create and manage a session cookie that allows the developers to create complex interaction features in their products.

Some steps into the workflows

A **workflow** is a sequence of predefined operations assigned to the system, to a user, or to a user group, that have to be executed in a predefined order.

This functionality can be used—for example—to create an approval procedure for articles, or to notify a user when a particular event happens.

eZ Publish allows the creation of workflows, and assigns them to triggers in order to easily manage tasks and, moreover, to provide us with an API for creating custom workflows for our extensions.

The default workflow events

eZ Publish exposes five default workflow events:

- Approve
- Wait until date
- Multiplexer
- Simple Shipping
- Payment Gateway

All of these can be used together in a cascade to create complex behavior, or can be used one-by-one to provide simple event management.

Approve

The Approve event will block a particular section from being published. In this event, you can choose if a user (or group) can be excluded, and who will approve new content.

Wait until date

This event filter requires a date attribute to be present in the chosen object class. This event will override the default publishing date specified by a user with the one defined in the workflow.

Multiplexer

This filter is very useful for combining different workflows together. It can be used to filter sections, classes, or users that other workflows run against.

Simple Shipping

This is used to add, for example, a new value for shipping costs in the e-commerce site. This cost will be added to the total cost of goods that the user has purchased.

Payment Gateway

This filter is used to manage the logic behind a payment gateway. To work, it should be used in conjunction a third-party payment gateway extension.

Creating a notification workflow

We will now create a workflow that will allow a specific editor (the editor chief who inherits from the **Administrator group roles**) to approve new content that is published in the blog by others editors.

Notification workflow

If you want to create a workflow notification system, the easiest way is to download and install the **eZ Information** extensions from the eZ System Projects site.

You can find more information here:
`http://projects.ez.no/ezinformation`

As the first step, we have to open the **Setup** tab and go to the **Workflow** link at the bottom of the left-hand sidebar.

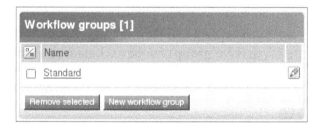

By default, eZ Publish creates an empty **Standard** workflow. We will open it and create a new workflow by using the **New workflow** button.

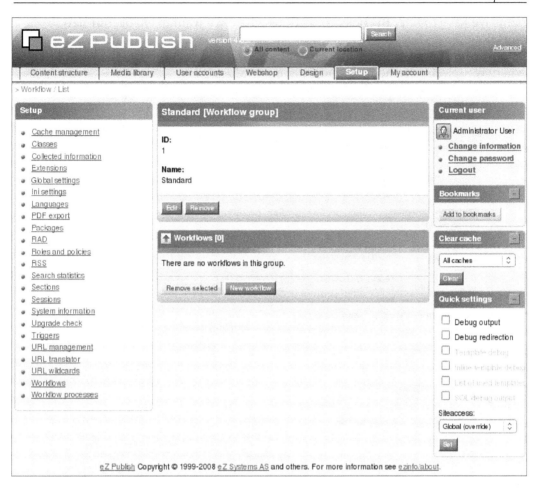

Next, we will compile the new workflow and name it as **Approve blog**. We will add an **Event / Multiplexer** choice from the select form by using the **Add event** button, as shown in the following screenshot:

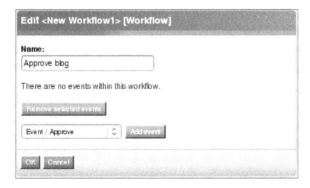

Now, we have to filter the objects/sections where we want to enable our new workflow. To do this, we have to complete the multiselect input fields, using the default value for all of the fields, except for **Classes**, in order to run the workflow, where we select both the **Blog** and **Blog post** values.

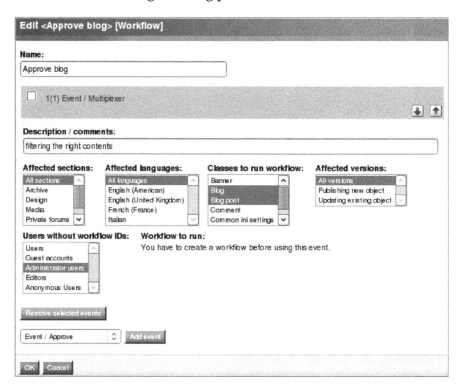

We will also select **Administrator users** in the **Users without workflow IDs** multiselect field, to make sure that the administrator's posts will not need to be approved.

After that, we have to create a new workflow based on an **approve event** filter. As before, create a new workflow inside the **Standard workflow** group by clicking on the **New workflow** button. Next, we will create a new event workflow, named **approving system**, by selecting **Event / Approve**.

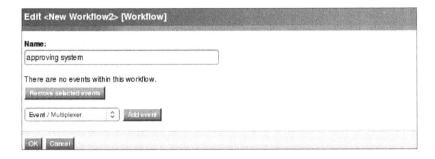

Because the blog doesn't belong to any particular section, we will choose the **All sections** value for the **Affected sections** form. We will not pay attention to the languages because we want to moderate all of them, but we will choose **Publishing new object** in the **Affected versions** area.

We have to enable the users or groups that need to approve the new content. We will choose the **Administrator users** group and also select this group in the following **Excluded user groups** area.

Next, we will save our new workflow by clicking on the **OK** button.

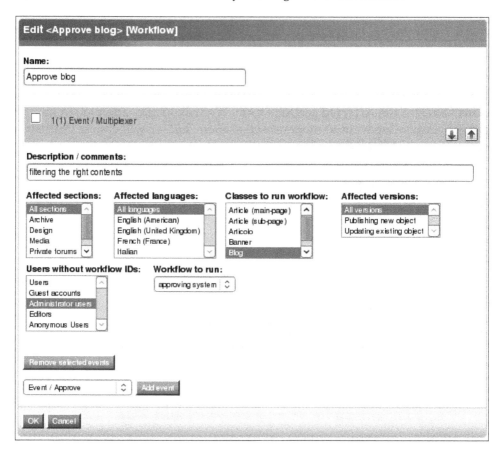

Next we have to re-edit the **Approve blog** workflow and select the **approving system** workflow as the **Workflow to run**. This will ensure that every time the **Approve blog** starts, the **approve** event will be executed for the correct object classes.

The next step is to assign our new **multiplexer workflow** to a particular event. To do this, we will use the **Triggers** function which is located in the menu of the **Setup** tab of the administration area.

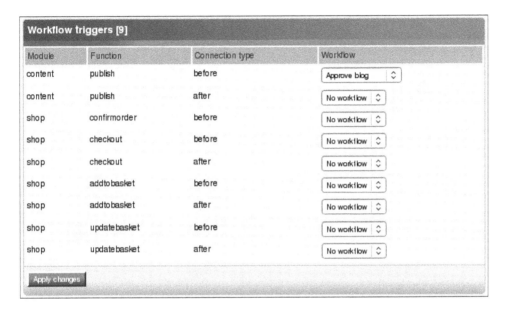

For the content module of the **publish before** function, we can now choose the workflow we just created (**Approve blog**). Next, we will click on the **Apply changes** button to enable it.

The workflow is enabled and every time that the editor tries to publish a new blog post, the new **Approve blog** workflow will be triggered and the user will see a message that alerts him or her that their new post is pending for approval. The administrator can then approve the new content from the **My account** tab from the **My pending items** link.

 The workflow engine works only in the background, and you can run it by adding the `/var/www/packtmediaproject/ezpublish.cron` file to your system crontab.

Summary

In this chapter, we learned how to manage eZ Publish users, groups, and permissions. We also reviewed what we did in the previous chapters and saw how the workflow system works. In the next chapter, we will see how the caching system works and how we can configure it.

11
Cache Configuration

Power is nothing without control

— Pirelli ads.

As we've seen so far, eZ Publish is a much advanced and powerful CMS and it needs to be well configured to work at its best. Like many other enterprise software applications, this CMF possesses an advanced caching system that is complex to set up and configure, but very powerful in the end. Configuring the caching system will help eZ Publish to perform better and reveal its strength.

In this chapter, we will see in detail, how such systems work, and will look at how to shape our site in order to make it the "Ferrari" of websites.

Caching system

Whenever we make a web request to a CMS that does not have a serious caching system, the web server is put under a severe test, as it has to perform the following things:

- Read the settings
- Query the database to retrieve the data requested
- Load the template
- Replace parsed variables with the required data
- Send everything to the client

The process, depending on the page complexity, could be very simple, or very heavy to perform.

A famous site with many concurrent requests, maybe even a powerful machine filled with RAM and CPUs will not be able to support so much work and cause the web server to hang.

The caching system is born to help the server to deploy applications more effectively.

 You can find some documentation on caching on Wikipedia at `http://en.wikipedia.org/wiki/Cache`.

Usually the bottleneck is caused by the query and template complexity. eZ Publish provides a system for caching at several levels:

- Template cache
- Template compile
- View cache

We will learn about each of these in detail in the coming sections.

Template cache

The template caching system provides the ability to cache static blocks of content and layout by using the {cache-block} template operator:

```
{cache-block [ keys=keys]
             [ expiry=expiry]
             [ ignore_content_expiry]
             [ subtree_expiry=subtree_expiry]}
...
{/cache-block}
```

This solution makes it possible to reduce the processing time of the main template (`pagelayout.tpl`), which often contains a lot of dynamic elements. It can be used to instruct the system to store and reuse cached blocks of template code based on different conditions.

- **Cache keys**: The `keys` parameter can be used to define the uniqueness of a cache block.
- **Time-based expiration**: The `expiry` parameter makes it possible to manually specify how long a cache block can live (as a number of seconds).
- **Content expiration**: By default, all the cache blocks expire when an object is published. If the `ignore_content_expiry` parameter is used, the cache block will not expire when an object is published.
- **Subtree expiration**: The `subtree_expiry` parameter can be used to bind the expiration of a cache block to a certain part of the content node tree.

eZ Webin cache block

eZ Webin provides a layout that is already set up with the correct cache-block. There are two large blocks, one for the header and another for the footer.

As we can see in this image, as recommended, there is a nested block inside the header that contains the logo, the menu, and a breadcrumb navigation menu.

 Breadcrumbs — or a breadcrumb trail — is a navigation aid used in user interfaces. It gives users a way to keep track of their location within programs or documents. The term comes from the trail of breadcrumbs left by Hansel and Gretel in the popular fairytale. For more information, go to `http://en.wikipedia.org/wiki/Breadcrumb_(navigation)`.

It's important to not put the `$module_result.content` variable in the cache block because it contains the main content of our pages. This is because the content of the actions of the modules are cached through other mechanisms.

To enable or disable the template cache system, you need to edit the `TemplateCache` setting of `TemplateSettings` section in the global or siteaccess `site.ini.append.php` file. If we enable the setting on the global setting file, it will be enabled for all our siteaccess. But if we enable it only in the siteaccess file, it will be enabled only for the related siteaccess.

```
[TemplateSettings]
...
TemplateCache=enabled
...
```

This code will enable the template cache. As a result, all of the cache block will be saved in `var/[siteaccess]/cache/template-block`.

Compiling a template

The eZ Publish template language, as with any meta language, needs to be parsed and interpreted by the CMS engine for any requests.

After activating the template compile functionality, all eZ Publish templates are processed and converted into real PHP language. In this way, the template can be directly interpreted without being parsed first.

To enable or disable this feature, we need to edit the `TemplateCompile` settings in the `TemplateSettings` section of the global siteaccess `site.ini.append.php` file, as shown below:

```
[TemplateSettings]
...
TemplateCompile=enabled
...
```

All compiled templates are saved in the `var/[siteaccess]/cache/template/compiled` folder.

Template optimization

If the `TemplateCompile` configuration is enabled, we can also enable the `TemplateOptimization` configuration. With this setting, eZ Publish will attempt to optimize the PHP code created, wherever possible.

Finally, there is another feature that greatly enhances the performance of CMS. This feature must be set via the `TemplateCompress` setting in the `TemplateSettings` section, as we can see in the following code:

```
[TemplateSettings]
...
TemplateCompress=enabled
...
```

Through this approach, it is possible to compress the PHP code into a binary code that interprets PHP much more rapidly.

View cache

The most important level of caching after the cache and compiled templates for layout is the view cache engine. This caching system is used to cache the output of the content module that is stored in the `$module_result.content` variable.

As mentioned above, this variable should never be placed inside the cache block, as it uses a different engine to cache the content.

To enable or disable this feature, we need to edit the `ViewCaching` setting in the `ContentSettings` section of the global or siteaccess `site.ini.append.php` file.

```
[ContentSettings]
...
ViewCaching=enabled
...
```

If we disable this setting, eZ Publish will never cache the content module output anymore.

This caching system works only for the "view" and "pdf" actions of the content module.

All cached content files are saved in the `var/[siteaccess]/cache/content` folder, and more than one file is created based on different parameters such as:

- User preferences
- User session
- View mode
- Language
- View parameters
- Layout

The `CachedViewModes` setting located in the `ContentSettings` section of the `site.ini` configuration file (or an override), controls view modes for which the caching will be enabled. The default value of this setting specifies that the view cache should be stored for the `full` and `sitemap` view modes, and the `pdf` view:

```
[ContentSettings]
...
CachedViewModes=full;sitemap;pdf
...
```

Enabling/Disabling the cache by context

If you need to disable view caching for a specific page, add the following line to the beginning of the template that is used:

```
{set-block scope=root variable=cache_ttl}0{/set-block}
```

This will set the `cache_ttl` global variable to zero (0) for the current template. The `cache_ttl` variable contains the **TTL** (Time to Live) value in seconds. The value `0` means that the result should not be changed. The value `-1` means that the view cache should never expire.

```
{set-block scope=root variable=cache_ttl}-1{/set-block}
```

Often, there is some relationship between the various caching siteaccesses. For example, if we delete the content cache of the administration panel, it's most likely that we would also want to delete the cache content of the frontend site.

To do this, we need to use the `RelatedSiteAccessList` setting in the `SiteAccessSettings` section of the `site.ini` global file (or override) setting, which controls what other siteaccesses must remove the cache content when emptying the cache. If this setting is not set, the system will use the `AvailableSiteAccessList`.

For example, we have the following `RelatedSiteAccessList` in our project directives:

```
[SiteAccessSettings]
. . .
RelatedSiteAccessList[]=ezwebin_site
RelatedSiteAccessList[]=eng
RelatedSiteAccessList[]=fre
RelatedSiteAccessList[]=ita
RelatedSiteAccessList[]=ezwebin_site_admin
. . .
```

Clearing the view cache

Every time you publish a new object or modify an existing one, the system automatically deletes the cache of some of the objects related to the published object including:

- All of the nodes associated with the published object
- All of the parents of the published object
- All of the nodes that contain the same keywords, if the "keywords" datatype is used on the published object
- All of the related nodes of the published object
- All of the related nodes of the published object with an "embed" tag

You can set the default behavior of deleting the caching system through the `ClearRelationTypes` setting on the `ViewCacheSettings` section of the `viewcache.ini.append.php` global (or override) file.

You can manually clear the cache of a node or a subtree either from the control panel, or via a shell script.

From the administration panel, navigate to the node for which you want to delete the cache, and then click on the icon near the name.

A pop-up window with a context menu will appear. Click on the **Delete view cache** link if you want to delete the cache for this node, or click on the **Delete view cache from here** link if you want to delete the cache for all of the subtree.

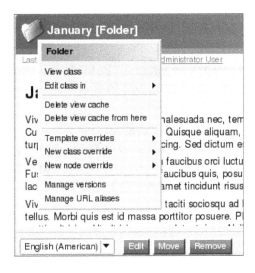

With the exception of the control panel, you can also delete the cache via the shell script.

For example, if you made changes to the template of the node with ID 81, which is equivalent to the `Issue-archive/2009/January` object, and the view cache is enabled, you will not be able to see the new changes until you clear the cache. To do this:

1. Navigate to the directory of your eZ Publish installation

2. Run the command

   ```
   ./bin/php/ezcontentcache.php –clear-node=81
   ```

   or

   ```
   ./bin/php/ezcontentcache.php –clear-node=/Issue-archive/
   2009/January
   ```

If you want to remove multiple nodes, they must be separated by commas, for example:

```
./bin/php/ezcontentcache.php –clear-node=81,82,83
```

To delete everything under the tree run the command:

```
./bin/php/ezcontentcache.php –clear-subtree=81
```

or

```
./bin/php/ezcontentcache.php –clear-subtree=/Issue-archive/2009/January
```

Smart cache

The smart cache system is a system developed to delete the cache between related objects. Using this system, you can define deleting rules in order to extend the default deleting system.

When we install a "white label" version of eZ Publish, this directive is turned off. But in our case, if we install a package as eZ Webinar, it is already enabled and configured for the custom package classes.

To enable or disable this configuration, you need to use the `SmartCacheClear` setting in the `ViewCacheSettings` section of the global (or override) `viewcache.ini.append.php` file. You can find this file in the `settings/override/` or `settings/siteaccess/<your_siteaccess>` directory.

```
[ViewCacheSettings]
...
SmartCacheClear=enabled
...
```

Once enabled, you can configure the custom `.ini` sections with custom-caching directives.

Let's take an example. In our project, when we publish a new issue, we want the **issue archive** page automatically to be updated to show the latest issue inserted and updated in the issue archive box, and its thumbnail in the right-hand sidebar.

As there is no direct relationship between the issue archive that belongs to the folder class and the new issue that belongs to the same class, it would not be possible to empty the issue's cache archive when we create or edit a new issue. This happens because the issue is not the issue's parent, a related object, or a class that shares the same keywords with the published issue.

Instead, through the mechanism of smart cache, we can set a custom section in our viewcache.ini global file in the settings/override/ directory, as follows:

```
[folder]
DependentClassIdentifier[]
DependentClassIdentifier[]=folder
MaxParents=2
ClearCacheMethod[]
ClearCacheMethod[]=object
```

In this way, when we empty the cache of a folder object, the system will also empty the cache of all of the folders that are its parents (to a maximum of two levels) or children. This will raise the content object tree, starting from the path_string level **node attribute**.

For our project, all of the eZ Webin settings we talked about so far are sufficient to meet our requirements for cache cancellation.

The following table depicts all of the rules that we can set in the custom smart cache section.

Name	Type	Description
DependentClassIdentifier	An array of class identifiers (not ID numbers)	Specifies which content classes will be considered as "dependent classes". If a node encapsulating an object of such a class is listed in path_string, svcs will add it to the list of additional nodes. The view cache for additional nodes will be cleared using the method(s) specified in the next setting.

Name	Type	Description
ClearCacheMethod	An array of strings	Defines which method(s) to use when clearing the view cache for additional nodes. This setting is an array of strings, where only six predefined values can be used. These are:
		Object: Clears the view cache for all of the locations (nodes) of the object.
		Parent: Clears the view cache for the parent node(s) of the object.
		Relating: Clears the view cache for related and reverse-related objects that have relations of the "common" type, and reverse-related objects that have relations of the "XML embedded" type (according to the "ClearRelationTypes" configuration setting).
		Keyword: Clears the view cache for the objects that have the same keyword as this object.
		Siblings: Clears the view cache for all of the siblings of this node/object.
		All: Clear the view cache for all of the listed methods above.
ObjectFilter	An array of object ID numbers	If specified, the view caches will only be cleared for those additional nodes that encapsulate the objects with these identifiers. If not specified, all of the additional nodes will have their view cache cleared.
MaxParents	Integer	Sets how many parents in path_string will be checked. If not specified, svcs will scan all of the parents listed in path_string.
AdditionalObjectIDs	An array of object ID numbers	Makes it possible to clear the caches for a set of arbitrary objects, regardless of whether their locations are listed in the node's path_string attribute or not.

Default caching settings

In the default configuration, all of the major levels of caching are enabled. If you install a "white label" eZ Publish, the only level not enabled by default is the *Smart Cache*, which needs to be configured manually, as seen in the previous section.

When we develop our project, it is very inconvenient to have the `ContentCache` setting enabled. This is because it means that we have to delete it every time we want to see the changes that we applied to a template.

To solve this problem, you can enable the `DevelopmentMode` setting in the `TemplateSettings` section of the global (or override) `site.ini` file that performs many more checks on the cancellation time of a template. But that directive is effective only on the content's cache, and not on the layout cache block.

If you want to disable the cache in an absolute way, you must add the following configuration settings to the global (or siteaccess) `site.ini.append.php` file:

```
[ContentSettings]
ViewCaching=disabled

[TemplateSettings]
NodeTreeCaching=disabled
TemplateCache=disabled
TemplateCompile=disabled
TemplateCompression=disabled
TemplateOptimization=disabled
```

In the following table, you will find the meaning of all of these settings:

Name	Value	Description
ViewCaching	enabled / disabled	Enable or disable the content object cache for the view action of the content module.
NodeTreeCaching	enabled / disabled	Enable or disable the caching of the nodetree.
TemplateCache	enabled / disabled	Enable or disable the possibility to cache all of the code's parts that use the {cache-block} template function.
TemplateCompile	enabled / disabled	Enable or disable the compiling of the template's codes in the PHP code.
TemplateCompression	enabled / disabled	Enable or disable the compression of the compiled template's code.
TemplateOptimization	enabled / disabled	Enable or disable the optimization of the compiled template's code.

Advanced eZ Publish caching system

Sometimes the standard caching levels are not sufficient to satisfy the requests to the site.

If this happens, first of all we should try to fine-tune all of the single views of our application, and then use other caching tools.

Advanced settings

The CMS supports other caching directives to store other system components in faster memory. By enabling these advanced settings, we can speed up the performance of eZ Publish CMS, because these settings can optimize its behavior in complex tasks, such as choosing the template to load based on overriding rules, generating the caching for content objects, reading the translation files or the user roles, and so on.

Override cache

Override cache is the setting that enables or disables the override templates rules caching.

To enable it, set the `Cache` settings in the `OverrideSettings` section of the global (or override) `site.ini` file to `enable`.

```
[OverrideSettings]
...
Cache=disabled
...
```

Pre-generation cache

Pre-generation cache is the setting that enables or disables the possibility to cache content when the object is published, and not at the first object request.

To enable it, set the `PreViewCache` setting of the `ContentSettings` section in the global (or override) `site.ini` file to `enable`.

```
[ContentSettings]
...
PreViewCache=enabled
...
```

Translation cache

Translation cache is the setting to enable or disable the translation file caching.

To enable it, set the `TranslationCache` setting of the `RegionalSettings` section of the global (or override) `site.ini` file to `enable`.

```
[RegionalSettings]
...
TranslationCache=enabled
...
```

Role cache

Role cache is the setting that enables or disables the users' roles caching.

To enable or disable it, set `EnableCaching` of the `RoleSettings` section of the global (or override) `site.ini` file to `true`.

```
[RoleSettings]
...
EnableCaching=true
...
```

Static cache

If we realize that there are many sections in our site (nodes or trees) with a very low upgrade frequency, and that they do not have dynamic parts, in accordance with the user preferences, we can generate static cache for them through eZ Publish.

Through this feature, the static HTML files are physically generated on the file system and then they will be served using the Apache rewrite rules, rather than requesting something from the CMS caching system.

To enable the static cache feature, it needs to be set in the `StaticCache` settings in the `ContentSettings` section of the global `site.ini` file.

```
[ContentSettings]
...
StaticCache=enabled
...
```

Now, we need to add new rewrite rules to the .htaccess file or the virtual host apache configuration:

```
RewriteEngine On

RewriteCond  /var/www/packtmediamagazine/static/index.html -f
RewriteRule ^$                  /static/index.html [L]
RewriteCond  %{REQUEST_METHOD}        !^POST$
RewriteCond  /var/www/packtmediamagazine/static$1/index.html -f
RewriteRule  ^(.*)$ /static$1/index.html [L]
RewriteRule !\.(gif|css|jpg|png|jar|ico|js)$ /index.php
```

These rules will tell Apache to forward all of the requested objects to a static generated file, except for the images.

Subsequently, we set some settings in the global staticcache.ini.append.php file.

```
[CacheSettings]
HostName=packtmediamagazine
StaticStorageDir=static
MaxCacheDepth=4
# A list of url's to cache
CachedURLArray[]=/*
```

Here, HostName is the domain name of our website, StaticStorage is the name of the directory where static files are generated, MaxCacheDepth shows how deep you must create static files in the tree, and CachedURLArray is an array rule of the path that we have cached.

Finally, to generate static files, go to a shell of our installation of eZ Publish and run the following command:

php bin/php/makestaticcache.php -s [siteaccess_name]

Here, [siteaccess_name] is the siteaccess name involved in this operation.

Opcode cache

When we use complex software, such as eZ Publish, for an enterprise website, where performances must be the best, it's very important to install software to optimize our PHP code.

There are several optimization code applications in the market and they are all open source. Some examples are:

- APC (http://pecl.php.net/package/APC)
- Zend Server (http://www.zend.com/products/server)
- eAccelerator (http://eaccelerator.net)
- XCache (http://xcache.lighttpd.net/)

Several benchmarks show the APC opcode accelerator as being the best solution for use with the CMF. It is available as a module for PHP and is easily configurable.

In the next chapter, we will see how to install this module in major Linux distributions.

You can check if you have an optimizer pre-installed in your system from the control panel of eZ Publish. To do this:

1. Log in to the site backend.
2. Click on the **Setup** link in the top menu.
3. Click on the **System information** link in the left-hand menu.
4. In the **PHP Accelerator** section, we can see which opcode is installed.

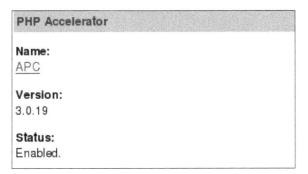

Proxy and HTTP Accelerator

You can also use reverse proxy systems for cache requests to eZ Publish. As with the opcode, there are various proxy software applications that can meet your needs. The most famous are:

- Squid (http://www.squid-cache.org)
- Varnish (http://varnish.projects.linpro.no)

Both of these are very powerful, but are also complicated to configure. To use them, we suggest contacting (or having in your team) an experienced system administrator who understands this software.

To manage the Varnish proxy, you should take a look at the open source eZ Publish extension at `http://projects.ez.no/all2evcc`.

To find some useful system information and gain control over granular caches, we suggest visiting the extension, `http://projects.ez.no/ggsysinfo`.

Customize cache settings to speed up the performance

In this section, we will summarize the configuration settings for caching of a quick site using eZ Publish.

In the global (or siteaccess) `site.ini` file, we need to have the following settings enabled:

```
[RegionalSettings]
...
TranslationCache=enabled
...
[ContentSettings]
...
ViewCaching=enabled
PreViewCache=enabled
...
[TemplateSettings]
...
NodeTreeCaching=enabled
TemplateCache=enabled
TemplateCompile=enabled
TemplateCompression=enabled
TemplateOptimization=enabled
...
[OverrideSettings]
...
Cache=enabled
...
[RoleSettings]
...
EnableCaching=true
UserPolicyCache=enabled
...
```

Next, in the global `viewcache.ini` (or override) file, we need to have the following settings:

```
[ViewCacheSettings]
ClearRelationTypes[]=common
ClearRelationTypes[]=reverse_common
ClearRelationTypes[]=reverse_embedded
ClearRelationTypes[]=reverse_attribute
SmartCacheClear=enabled
```

Moreover, as we said, the installation of an opcode accelerator like APC is also strongly recommended.

What not to do in a template

The Achilles' heel of eZ Publish is the template system subframework that cannot, and should not, be overrated, and that is used as a true programming language.

For this reason, we should not have templates with very complex logic. The templates should only render HTML data, and not involve any kind of business logic.

If the predefined objects of eZ Publish that we can use in our templates are not sufficient to publish the data that we want to represent, we should move the business logic either inside an operator or function, or create a new module.

A classic error that many developers make is to perform many queries in a single template file. It is not recommended to have more than two queries within the same template. If we need more than two queries we have to use a template operator or a custom fetch function, which are much faster to execute.

For example, if we have to print the children of a node, we should use the `$node.children` attribute, rather than making a new query that returns `childrens`.

The following code should not be used:

```
{$childrens=fetch(content, list, hash(parent_node_id, $node.node_id))}
{foreach $childrens as $children}
  {node_view_gui view=line content_node=$children}
{/foreach}
```

This must be replaced with the following:

```
{foreach $node.children as $children}
 {node_view_gui view=line content_node=$children}
{/foreach}
```

In this way, we optimize the template performance because we don't use the `fetch` function in the template, but the `children` attribute of the node, which decreases the query's number.

Another trick is to limit and page the template queries, to reduce the database load:

```
{fetch( 'content', 'list', hash('parent_node_id', 2,
        'limit', 15, 'offset', 10) )}
```

The content list `fetch` function takes two parameters: `limit` and `offset`. The `limit` parameter sets the item number to be listed, whereas the `offset` parameter sets the first element from where the query starts.

In conclusion, wrong templates are those where:

- Business logic is created through the template language instead of through PHP code
- There are more than two template queries
- There are template queries that can be replaced by ready-made attributes of the node object
- Template queries are not limited and not paginated

Summary

In this chapter, we saw how to use the eZ Publish system cache. We saw the three caching levels, including advanced features, such as smart cache clear.

Correctly configuring the caching system in an enterprise-class CMS is complex, and very important because, in order to support many web requests, there isn't any other way than have a good caching system.

In the next chapter, we will see how to deploy our site to a production server and how to manage it remotely.

12
Deployment

Who sings on Friday, will weep on Sunday.

— A proverb

It's time to deploy our site! In the previous chapter, we finished working on the site and now, in this chapter, we will understand the differences between the development, staging, and production environments. We will then deploy our development environment to a production server, by using the eZ Deploy extension. We will also use the Selenium IDE to create a functional test for quality assurance.

Environments

When we work on an enterprise application, it is always useful to work in three separate environments:

- Development environment
- Staging environment
- Production environment

Basically, an environment is a server configured for specific purposes (for example, to allow users to use a site or develop a new one).

You can also add more environments, such as **Integration platform environment**, where different teams would test if their code works fine together; usually, only these three are really needed.

Development environment

This first environment is the one in which we will work. Usually, this environment has installed libraries useful for a development task, such as XDebug PHP module, but is totally useless, or even problematic, in a production server. For example, an enabled XDebug PHP module will slow down our production server, while adding overhead to every PHP execution. If you don't have a development server, this environment should be the computer where you create your whole application.

Staging environment

This environment is used to test the site, or the latest features, on a server that is basically a clone of the production one. The staging server is normally used to run all of the quality assurance and performance tests. For this reason, it's very important that both the staging and the production environments use the same libraries, and have the same configuration. This will ensure that when we deploy to the production server, everything will go according to our plans. Sometimes, to reduce the deployment costs for small sites, the staging server is the same as the production server. But in this case, performance tests have to be done on the development server to avoid slowing down the site.

Production environment

The last environment is the production environment. In this environment, users will find the site reachable and usable. For this reason, it is very important that it has to be secured and that all of the development stuff, and any unused libraries have been removed.

Moreover, a single server is not always sufficient to host a popular site. Sometimes it is necessary to separate and clone the database and the HTTP servers on different machines, as shown in the following figure:

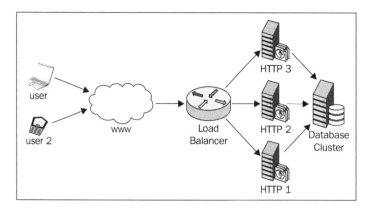

The production environment should be completely different from the staging or the development one. Basically, it should be a single machine or a virtual machine. As we can see in the previous figure, the production environment uses a load balancer to distribute the work across different HTTP servers and a single (or clustered) database server.

Preparing the production server

As we don't need to install eZ Publish again as we did in the first two chapters, we will now concentrate on the PHP configuration of our machine. As we said before, a production server should have only the libraries strictly necessary. We have to remove, or disable, the unused libraries from either the package manager of our distribution (`yum` for Red Hat based distributions or `apt-get` for Debian based distributions), or from the `PHP.ini` file.

As we saw in Chapter 1, our eZ Publish site requires only the default PHP libraries, plus the **php5-GD** and **ImageMagik** applications and libraries. Moreover, as we saw in the last chapter, to reach the best performance from the PHP interpreter, an opcode cache system such as **APC** should be installed. As we will see next, we will also need a **Secure Shell Daemon** (**SSHD**) and a rsync client, to enable the deploy process.

As this book does not cover the specific system administration tasks, we again suggest that you work with a Linux system administrator to optimize the production server.

Deploying an eZ Publish site

Software deployment involves all of the activities that make a software system available for use on a particular environment.

There are different ways to deploy software, such as using an FTP client or using SSH and rsync.

With eZ Publish, the suggested activities to deploy a website are:

1. Download **eZ Deploy** extension from `http://projects.ez.no/ezsync`.
2. Create a quality assurance test with automatic (**SeleniumIDE** + **PHPUnit**), or manual processes for all of the functionality that we developed.
3. Configure the staging siteaccess with the correct settings.
4. Deploy the database in the staging environment.

5. Deploy the code in the staging environment.

6. Check the validity of the staging server.

7. Run quality assurance tests in the staging environment.

8. Repeat steps 3, 4, 5, 6, 7 on the production server.

Each of the above steps are covered in the following sections.

eZ Deploy

We have to download and install the extension called **eZ Deploy**. We will use this extension to synchronize the different environments with the latest code that we created. To download the extension, we have to check out the code from the public repository, by using a subversion client.

 Usually, Subversion is installed by default in all of the modern Linux distributions, but you can also download it from `http://subversion.tigris.org/`.

`cd /var/www/packtmediaproject/`

`svn export http://svn.projects.ez.no/ezsync/trunk extension/ezsync`

Here, we have to enable the extension from the global `site.ini` file located in the `settings` folder:

`vi settings/override/site.ini.append.php`

Add the following lines:

```
[ExtensionSettings]
ActiveExtensions[]=packtmedia

...

ActiveExtensions[]=ezsync
```

Note that eZ Deploy should work in order to install it in the production and staging environment of both the SSH and rsync servers. Later in this chapter, we will see how to configure the extension in order to make it work.

Creating the automatic tests

This step isn't mandatory. However, to be certain that the site will run without any glitches on the staging server, we should perform some assurance tests by using software such as Selenium IDE, and then run them automatically by using Selenium RC and PHPUnit.

One of the best software applications for fulfilling this task is Selenium (`http://seleniumhq.org`). This is a quality assurance suite based on a remote control written in Java, and on an IDE that can manage different browsers on different machines.

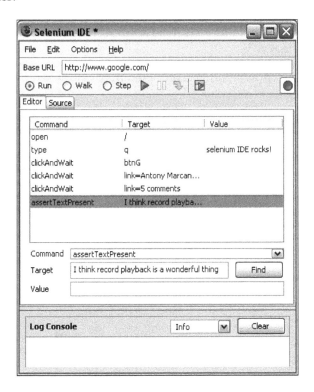

As we can see here, the IDE is a Firefox plugin that allows us to record a navigation session and export it in different formats so that it is reproduced automatically by a test framework such as PHPUnit (`http://www.phpunit.de`).

The PHPUnit will then use the Selenium RC (Selenium Remote Control) to run the tests and create a complete report about them.

In the official PHPUnit documentation, you can read how to integrate and use it with Selenium, at `http://www.phpunit.de/manual/3.4/en/selenium.html`.

Installing the Selenium IDE

The Selenium IDE (Integrated Development Environment) is a tool that you can use to develop your Selenium test cases. It's a Firefox plugin and is generally the most efficient way to develop test cases.

It also allows us to save all of our tests in a useful test suite, or to export it in the PHPUnit test format.

To install it, we have to download it, using the Firefox browser, from `http://seleniumhq.org/download/`.

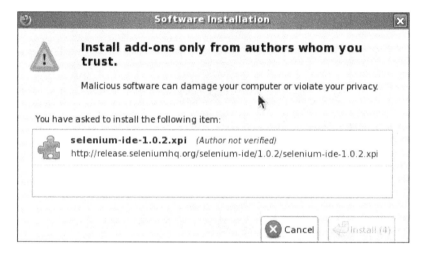

Now, as we can see in this screenshot, Firefox will ask us to install the new component and then restart it in order to use the new extension.

Recording a session

We can now use the Selenium IDE to record our first test session. We will see how to create a simple test, but you can play with the IDE to make the best use of all of its features.

Open your browser , and navigate to the site URL (in our case,
`http://packtmediaproject`). In the **Tools** menu of Firefox, select the
Selenium IDE option, as shown here:

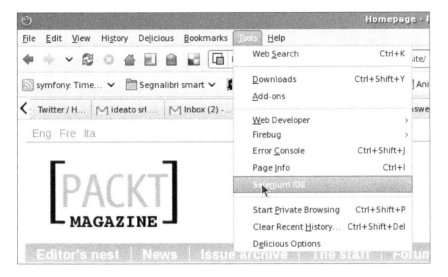

The IDE will then open, and we can start recording our session by clicking on the
record button (in red) located on the rightmost side of the IDE window, as seen here:

Now every time we use the browser Selenium, we will record our actions to create a
test. For example, we will test the Forum to see if it works correctly.

Click on the **Forum** link in the navigation menu of the site, and take a look at the IDE to see what it has registered:

As you can see in the previous screenshot, Selenium recorded an open action for the index and a click on the link. The **clickAndWait** command means that the IDE will wait for a complete render of the page from the browser before testing its content.

Customizing tests

Browsing a site with Selenium should be sufficient in most cases, but sometimes you also need to check for the page contents. Starting from the previous test, we will extend it to check to see if the page contains the forum we created.

Now, stop the recording and choose the **assertText** command in the **Command** select box of the IDE. This will be used to confirm the existence of a string in the **XPath** position. Now, in the **Target** input area, we have to specify the **XPath** path where we want to check the text filled, in the **Value** field.

XPath is used to navigate through elements and attributes in an XML document. XPath is a major element in the W3Cs XSLT standard, and XQuery and XPointer are both built on XPath expressions. You can learn how to use XPath from the W3School tutorials site at `http://www.w3schools.com/XPath/`.

As you can see in our example screenshot, we have to check that the forum name is **Tech and gadgets**.

Save your test from the **File** menu and play it using the **Play current test case** button, to check if everything is fine, as shown in the following screenshot:

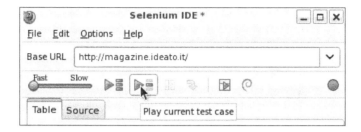

We suggest that you create as many tests like this as possible to cover all of the pages of the site, which would assure good quality assurance coverage.

To create useful tests, read the Selenium IDE documentation and tutorial at `http://seleniumhq.org/docs/03_selenium_ide.html#building-test-cases`.

Configuring the staging and production siteaccesses

As we saw in Chapter 2, when we created the siteaccess, we had to create different siteaccesses for different environments. So far, we used only the development siteaccess. But now we have to configure the staging and production siteaccesses.

To do that, we have to be sure that all of the cache settings we discussed in the previous chapter are enabled, and that the databases and other settings (site URL, regional settings, and so on) are configured accordingly, for the staging or production servers.

We can check everything from the `site.ini.append.php` file which can be found in the `settings/siteaccess/staging` and `settings/siteaccess/staging_panel` directories of the eZ Publish installation.

Moreover, in the same `site.ini.append.php` file, we have to disable debugging in both environments by changing the `Debug` value from `enabled` to `disabled`.

```
[DebugSettings]
Debug=disabled
```

Deploying the database

After we create the test and check the siteaccesses configuration, we can start with the *real deploy* process.

First, we have to copy the development database to the staging server. To do this, we have to create a dump file of the development database and then restore it onto the staging server.

If you didn't change the username and the password of the MySQL user, you make this copy by using the following commands:

```
cd ~
mysqldump packtmediaproject -upacktuser -ppacktpwd > packtmediadump.sql
```

After we copy the generated `packmediadump.sql` to the new server, we have to execute the following shell command to restore the dump:

```
mysqlimport packtmediaproject -upacktuser -ppacktpwd /path/to/
packtmediadump.sql
```

If you change the name of the database, the username, or the password of the database user in the previous step, then you need to use the correct ones.

Deploying the code

To copy the development files to the staging server, we will use the eZ Deploy extension. This extension was specifically created for this kind of tasks, and uses the rSync protocol to send and synchronize the code from one server to another. The extension will send the files incrementally, so that only the changed files will be sent from one deployment to another.

Configuring the extension

We have to configure the extension so that it works with the servers where we want to deploy the files. To do this, we have to edit the `sync.ini.append.php` file located in the `settings` directory of the extension.

```
cd /var/www/packtmediaproject/extension/ezsync
vi settings/sync.ini.append.php
```

Let's suppose that we have the staging server in a subdomain of the `packtmediamagazine.com` domain, and then add the following lines:

```
[DefaultSyncSettings]
Host=
Dir=
User=
Port=22
Parameters=
FileRsyncEclude=extension/ezsync/settings/rsync_exclude.txt

[StagingSyncSettings]
Dir=/var/www/staging
Host=staging.packtmediamagazine.com
User=packtmedia

[ProductionSyncSettings]
Dir=/var/www/production
Host=www.packtmediamagazine.com
User=packtmedia
```

As you can see, the `StagingSyncSettings` section is used to configure the staging server, whereas the `ProductionSyncSettings` section is used for the production server. If you want to create other environments, you should easily create new deployment configurations by adding new sections.

The `Dir` parameter specifies the remote directory where rSync will place the files, the `Host` is the remote server to contact, and the `User` is the SSH user that will have write permission on the `Dir` directory.

Excluding files from deploy

We should also exclude files from the synchronization directories, or files that are used only in the development process, or that are generated by the CMF cache system. To do so, we have to edit the file named `rsync_exclude.txt`, which can be found inside the extension `settings` directory.

```
cd /var/www/packtmediaproject/extension/ezsync
vi settings/rsync_exclude.txt
```

We need to add the names of the files and directory that we want to exclude, by editing the `rsync_exclude.txt` file and adding the following lines:

```
.svn
var/*
update
doc
```

This will ensure that, on the staging or production server, we will not copy the subversion directories, the local cache, the update script, and all the documentation we created for internal development that is not suitable for publishing on the Web.

Starting the synchronization

After configuring the extension, we have to move back to the root of the eZ Publish installation and execute the sync script in the *dry-run mode*:

cd /var/www/packtmediaproject/

php extension/ezsync/bin/php/sync.php --env=staging

The dry-run mode will not send anything, but it will show us which files will be sent during the real deployment. To execute this, we have to add the `--go` parameter to the shell script:

php extension/ezsync/bin/php/sync.php --env=staging --go

Now the site has been deployed to the staging server.

Checking the validity

After we have deployed the code, we need to check if we have configured the server and the CMF correctly. Luckily, eZ Publish will help us to do this, through its **Check Validity** functionality. To enable this feature (which will again run the configuration wizard that we saw in Chapter 1), we have to set the `CheckValidity` parameter to `true` in the `SiteAccessSettings` section of the main `site.ini` file:

cd /var/www/packtmediaproject/

vi settings/site.ini

Now, in the file add the following code:

```
[SiteAccessSettings]
...
CheckValidity=true
...
```

Now, we can check to see if the staging installation is working correctly, by browsing the site itself and taking a look at the configuration wizard, which we used to configure eZ Publish in Chapter 1. To do that, we have to open the browser on the staging server URL and follow the configuration wizard instructions as shown here:

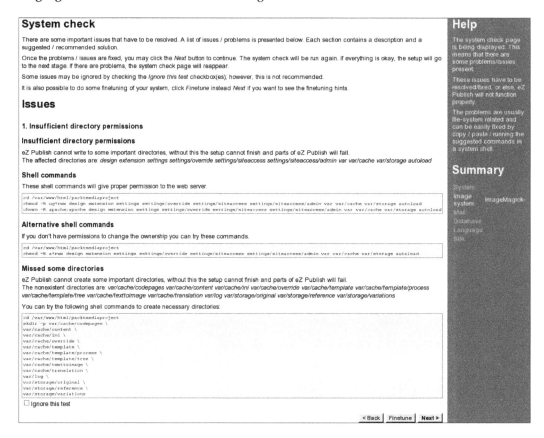

As we can see in the screenshot, if something goes wrong, the wizard will help us to fix the problem, step-by-step. After we have checked that everything works fine, we need to change the `CheckValidity` parameter back to `false`, and reload the site.

Quality assurance

Now, we can run all of the acceptance tests that we created previously, to confirm that all of the functionality works fine. To automatically run the test, we should install the Selenium Remote Control on the staging server, instead of using the IDE.

 The Selenium RC guide can be found on the Selenium project site at `http://seleniumhq.org/projects/remote-control/`.

Deploying to the production server

After we check that everything works smoothly on the staging server, we can deploy the site to production. To synchronize to the production server, we will execute the following script:

```
php extension/ezsync/bin/php/sync.php -env=production --go
```

After the synchronization, as we saw previously, check the validity, run the acceptance tests and that's all. Now it's time to publicize the site to our customers!

Summary

In this chapter, we saw what environments are, and the best practices for creating them. We also learned how to deploy a site to different environments, which software is the best for performing quality assurance, and how to create some functional tests by using Selenium IDE software. We also learned how to use the eZ Deploy extension to fulfill this task. In the next chapter, we will look at some useful tips for using eZ Publish.

A
APC Installation and Optimization

During the creation of a site, we discussed a lot of things not directly related to it, but very useful in our job. In this chapter, we will see how to apply some of these concepts and understand how the others work. We will also look at some of the best extensions developed by the eZ Publish community.

APC tuning for eZ Publish

We have discussed APC, both in the cache chapter and in the previous. Now, we will understand better what it is and how it works.

Opcode Cache

To publish the web pages, eZ Publish has to elaborate on a lot of data. In some cases, this work could turn out to be a CPU-eater and thus slow down the response of the server. For this reason, it is useful to install and use an opcode cache system such as APC. This kind of system will save the PHP intermediate code that is generated by the PHP interpreter in memory, and re-use it when called by the interpreter.

How does it work?

As we can see in the following schema, the page requests are first analyzed, to see if they are declared as either cacheable or not. If they are cacheable, the system will check to see if there is suitable content in the cache, or if it has to create (and save) a new one.

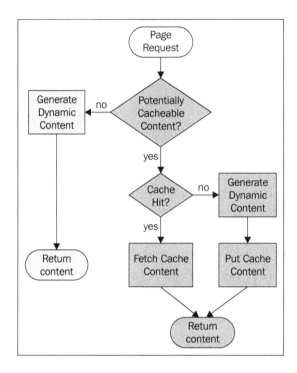

Installing APC

To install APC, we have to be sure that our Linux server has the necessary packages to compile it.

These packages are related to the building system (GCC, Make, Glibc, and so on), that is, the development headers for Apache and PHP.

If our distribution is a derivation of GNU Linux Debian (like Ubuntu), we can install it using `apt-get`, by using the root account or a user in the sudoers group.

```
sudo apt-get install build-essential
sudo apt-get install php5-dev apache2-dev
```

Otherwise, if we have a Red Hat based distribution (such as Fedora or CentOS), we have the building packages installed by default. We only need to install the PHP and Apache development packages, by using a root account.

```
yum install php-devel httpd-devel
```

Installing from sources

After we are sure that we have all of the required packages, we can execute the following commands from a shell, in order to download and compile APC from the source code:

```
cd /usr/local/src
wget http://pecl.php.net/get/APC
tar -xzf APC-x.x.x.tgz
cd APC-x.x.x
phpize
./configure –enable-apc-mmap
make
sudo make install
```

PECL installation

Another way of installing APC is by using PECL. This is a module repository for PHP, with a lot of different modules. Moreover, when installed, PHP has a PECL shell command available by default, which can be used to install or remove modules.

As for the source code, we have to ensure that we have the PHP development packages before installing APC.

The installation should be done by a root user from the command line, by executing the following code:

```
pecl install apc
```

APC configuration

APC has a lot of features, all of them well explained in the online manual (http://php.net/manual/book.apc.php). We will now configure our installation to work with eZ Publish.

To do this, we have to create a file called `apc.ini`, and place it in the correct path in the base of the Linux flavor we are using:

- On GNU Linux Debian, we will create the file in `/etc/php5/conf.d/apc.ini`

- On Red Hat based distributions, we have to create the file in `/etc/php.d/apc.ini`

    Now, in the file we have to enter the following lines:

    ```
    # Load APC extension
    extension=apc.so
    apc.enabled = 1
    apc.shm_size=64
    apc.filters=cache
    apc.file_update_protection = "0"
    apc.include_once_override = "1"
    ```

Whereas the first two lines simply enable the module, the others are required to optimize APC for our purposes.

We will now describe this code, line by line:

- `apc.shm_size`: This defines the size of each shared-memory segment, in MB.

- `apc.filters`: This specifies a list of comma-separated values of regular POSIX expressions. If any pattern matches a source filename, that file will not be cached. In our case, we are configuring APC to not cache the eZ Publish cache.

- `apc.file_update_protection`: The `file_update_protection` parameter is used to lock the file for a certain time slot. By default, this time slot is two seconds, but we can also deactivate it (with the 0 value) if we are sure that our file will be accessed (or modified) with atomic instructions (as rsync does).

- `apc.include_once_override`: This value allows us to enable the optimizer for the PHP `require_once()` and `include_once()` functions, in order to avoid the expensive system call used.

APC GUI

If we install APC with PECL, we will find a file named `apc.php` in the `/usr/share/php` folder. This file can be used to analyze the APC works. To use it, we have to copy the file in the HTTP server directory (such as `/var/www/`) and then browse it using our preferred browser.

The result will be as shown here:

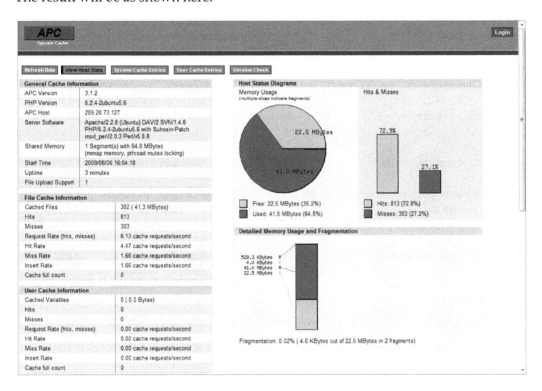

Other than the cache, with this script we can also check the memory usage to better configure the `shm_size` parameter for the server that we are using.

Performance

As a simple example, we will run the site with and without APC, on our development laptop, using ApacheBench Version 2.3 (http://httpd.apache.org/docs/2.2/programs/ab.html). Here are the results:

Without APC		With APC	
Concurrency Level:	5	Concurrency Level:	5
Time taken for tests: seconds	15.880	**Time taken for tests: seconds**	**8.112**
Complete requests:	100	Complete requests:	100
Failed requests:	43	Failed requests:	40
(Connect: 0, Receive: 0, Length: 43, Exceptions: 0)		(Connect: 0, Receive: 0, Length: 40, Exceptions: 0)	
Write errors:	0	Write errors:	0
Total transferred: bytes	3436775	Total transferred: bytes	3436371
HTML transferred: bytes	3379675	HTML transferred: bytes	3379271
Requests per second: [#/sec] (mean)	6.30	**Requests per second: [#/sec] (mean)**	**12.33**
Time per request: [ms] (mean)	794.005	**Time per request: [ms] (mean)**	**405.600**
Time per request: [ms] (mean, across all concurrent requests)	158.801	**Time per request: [ms] (mean, across all concurrent requests)**	**81.120**
Transfer rate: [Kbytes/sec] received	211.35	Transfer rate: [Kbytes/sec] received	413.69

By enabling APC, we can see that the execution time for running the tests is half, and that the requests for the second are twice that of the previous one.

B
Advance Debugging

During the development of an eZ Publish site, it is very important to have immediate feedback about what we are doing. The CMF gives us a couple of debuggers to help us in our task. These are the code debugger and the template debugger.

Code debugger

eZ Publish includes a wrapper for all of the errors returned by PHP, which will display the errors at the bottom of our page, or in a new page if we prefer. When we release a site, it's very important that all of the errors are fixed, in order to avoid bad surprises or a slowdown of the application.

To use the debugging capabilities of the system, we have to edit the `site.ini` file of the global siteaccess, and enable the `DebugOutput` parameter.

```
[DebugSettings]
DebugOutput=enabled
```

After we enable this setting and empty the cache, we will see the debugger, as shown in the following screenshot:

On this page, we can see some utils that are used to clear the cache and enable different kinds of debug, such as the loading the `.ini` files, the execution of the queries, or the template rendering time.

Moreover, this parameter will enable some special operators for the template that will allow us to print the HTML output of the page, and the values of the variables used.

Debug template operators

The most important operators for debugging are `debug-log`, `debug-timing-point`, and `debug-accumulator`. These operators allow us to see particular information about how much time our code needs to run, and the values of the instantiated variables. We will look at the operators one by one.

Debug-log

This operator will perform a PHP `var_dump` of objects, arrays, and strings. This means that you'll be able to see what a particular object contains in the current page.

```
{debug-log var=$object msg='object contents'}
{debug-log msg='hello world'}
{debug-log var=array(1,2,3)}
```

Debug-timing-point

This particular operator will give us the ability to analyze the time needed to execute a certain block of code.

```
{debug-timing-point id=""}
{$item} - {$item2}
{/debug-timing-point}
```

Timing points:

Checkpoint	Elapsed	Rel. Elapsed	Memory	Rel. Memory
Script start	0.0000 sec	0.0399 sec	780.8438 KB	1,096.8047 KB
Module start 'content'	0.0399 sec	0.0161 sec	1,877.6484 KB	721.5000 KB
Module end 'content'	0.0560 sec	0.0481 sec	2,599.1484 KB	849.2813 KB
End	0.1040 sec		3,448.4297 KB	
Total runtime:	0.5038 sec			
Peak memory usage:	10,078.0156 KB			

As we can see in the above screenshot, you can truncate your code with some checkpoints to see which parts of your templates are the most time-consuming.

Debug-accumulator

The debug-accumulator template function executes the body and generates the statistics. The number of calls, total time, and average time will be shown in the debugger.

```
{debug-accumulator}
{section var=error loop=$errors}{$error}{/section}
{/debug-accumulator}
```

Time accumulators:				
Accumulator	Elapsed	Percent	Count	Average
ini_load				
Load cache	0.0369 sec	7.1646%	13	0.0028 sec
FindInputFiles	0.0076 sec	1.4759%	13	0.0006 sec
Parse	0.0160 sec	3.0999%	2	0.0080 sec
Save Cache	0.0028 sec	0.5479%	2	0.0014 sec
Mysql Total				
Mysql_queries	0.0022 sec	0.4190%	3	0.0007 sec
Looping result	0.0002 sec	0.0348%	3	0.0001 sec
Template Total	0.4308 sec	83.6%	2	0.2154 sec
Template load	0.1803 sec	34.9792%	2	0.0902 sec
Template processing	0.2503 sec	48.5410%	2	0.1251 sec
String conversion in template resource	0.0002 sec	0.0471%	5	0.0000 sec
Template parser: create text elements	0.0071 sec	1.3857%	3	0.0024 sec
Template parser: remove whitespace	0.0016 sec	0.3103%	3	0.0005 sec
Template parser: construct tree	0.0406 sec	7.8806%	3	0.0135 sec
Template load and register function	0.0088 sec	1.7071%	3	0.0029 sec
override				
Cache load	0.0139 sec	2.6955%	2	0.0069 sec
General				
String conversion	0.0011 sec	0.2163%	15	0.0001 sec
INI string conversion	0.0013 sec	0.2456%	8	0.0002 sec
String conversion w/ mbstring	0.0008 sec	0.1644%	4	0.0002 sec
dbfile	0.0002 sec	0.0429%	4	0.0001 sec
Total script time:	**0.5156 sec**			

This operator is quite useful when we want to have a complete view of how complex the pages are and the resources that they need, such as MySQL query timing.

Templating debug

Using the debugger of the templating system, we should be able to know:

- The list of the templates and sub-templates loaded into the displayed page
- The number of these templates

- The total number of loaded templates, if some templates are loaded more than once

To enable this debugger, as shown in the previous screenshot, we have to enable the `debugOutput` option, as seen before. Next, we have to enable the `ShowUsedTemplates` setting of the `TemplateSettings`, in the same `site.ini` file.

```
[TemplateSettings]
...
ShowUsedTemplates=enabled
...
```

Moreover, by enabling this kind of debug, we'll be able to edit the templates by clicking on the **relative edit** button. You can see this in the following screenshot:

Now, we can enable the verbose debugger output, by using the Debug parameter, and then render the inline of the name of the loaded template in the HTML page, by using the ShowXHTMLCode parameter.

```
[TemplateSettings]
...
Debug=enabled
ShowXHTMLCode=enabled
...
```

When ShowXHTMLCode is enabled, eZ publish will display a comment in the rendered output of the browser each time a new template is loaded, as shown in the previous screenshot.

eZ Publish's Best Extensions

Many open-source CMSes, including eZ Publish, have a vibrant and active community that develops a lot of new extensions, site styles, and hacks. Some of them are really useful, whereas others are less useful. But in any case, you should visit the contrib repository (`http://ez.no/developer/contribs`) before starting to develop any functionality.

We will now describe the open source extensions taken from the eZ System project site (`http://projects.ez.no`) which we have used for developing some of our sites.

eZ Xajax

The eZ Xajax extension integrates the xajax PHP class library into eZ Publish. This extension is used to add Ajax functionality to the CMF, which is used by some other community extensions.

You can download eZ Xajax from: `http://projects.ez.no/ezxajax`.

Star Rating

Star Rating is an extension that allows the addition of a rating system to your eZ Publish content objects via a datatype. This extension uses Ajax calls through the xajax extension to save the vote without reloading the page, and checks the user's session to ensure that he or she doesn't vote more than once.

To use this extension, we only need to add the Star Rating attribute to the content class that we want to be rated, and update its view template.

This extension will be soon replaced by the eZ Star Rating (`http://projects.ez.no/ezstarrating`) that will use the new functionality of the forthcoming eZ Publish 4.2.

You can download Star Rating from `http://ez.no/developer/contribs/applications/star_rating`.

eZ Publish OE

eZ Publish Online Editor 5.0 is a replacement for Online Editor 4.x. It uses the tinyMCE editor, which means that it works on IE7 Vista, supports full-screen editing, provides resizable edit area, and a lot more, out of the box.

eZ Publish OE is very powerful and can be a valid substitute for the official WYSIWYG editor. It is included by default in the newer eZ Publish 4.1.x branch.

You can download eZ Publish OE from `http://projects.ez.no/ezoe`.

eZ JSCore

This is an Ajax extension, like eZ Xajax, and is useful for easier client/server integration. It makes use of YUI 3.0 and jQuery (not enabled by default).

You can download eZ JSCore from `http://projects.ez.no/ezjscore`.

Google Sitemaps

This extension creates an XML sitemap of an eZ Publish installation for the Google webmaster tools (`https://www.google.com/webmasters/tools/`) and other services, by using a cronjob.

You can download Google Sitemaps from `http://projects.ez.no/all2egooglesitemaps`.

eZ Deploy

We saw this extension in the Deployment chapter. eZ Deploy is an automatic deploy system based on the rsync shell script. It allows deploying an eZ application from the development environment to the production through the rsync system. As a limitation, this extension works only with complete privileges on the eZ Publish installation directory and needs a working rsync server on the production server.

You can download from `http://projects.ez.no/ezsync`.

Data Import

This is one of the most powerful extensions used. If you plan to migrate your site from a different CMS to eZ Publish, data import can be the solution for all of your questions. The purpose of the Data Import extension is to import data from a given data source (such as the `xml/csv` documents) into the eZ Publish content tree using an object-oriented approach. Developers need to implement a SourceHandler that understands the given datasource that is completely independent from the import operators. The import operators contain the logic of how to create/update the content nodes in eZ Publish.

You can download from `http://ez.no/developer/contribs/import_export/ data_import`.

Index

Symbols

$node 141
$node.data_map attribute 141
$node.data_map.profile_description.content.
    output.output_text attribute 142
$node.name attribute 141
$node.object.data_map attribute 141
$node.url_alias attribute 141
$versionview_mode variable 163
{attribute_view_gui attribute=$node.data_
    map. short_description} function 147
{literal} operator 108

A

Access Control List. *See* ACL
ACL 195
actions/, extension directory structure 91
AdditionalObjectIDs, smart cache 222
alignment 142
APC
  configuration 249, 250
  GUI 251
  installing 248, 249
  installing, from sources 249
  installing, PECL used 249
  opcode cache 247
  performance 252
  working 248
APC, configuration
  apc.file_update_protection 250
  apc.filters 250
  apc.include_once_override 250
  apc.shm_size 250

approve event, workflow event 205
article attributes, content class
  author 58
  body 58
  enable comments 58
  image 58
  intro 58
  keywords 58
  short title 58
  title 58
Article class
  extending 63, 64
article content class 50
  article objects, generating 50, 51
article, content tree
  comments, enabling 86
  creating 85
  publish and unpublish date 86
attributes, content class 58
attribute_view_gui function 141
authors.tpl template 147
autoloads/, extension directory structure 91
automatic tests, eZ Publish site
  creating 234, 235
  Selenium IDE, installing 236
  session, recording 236, 238
  tests, customizing 238, 239

B

backend
  about 68
  areas 68, 69
  content area 68
  navigation bar (on the top of the screen) 68

right menu 68
secondary menu (on the left of the screen) 68
backend activation, extension 97
backend, content structure 69
Balsamiq 113
bin, extension 90
bin/, extension directory structure 91
blog feed
  creating 176-179
breadcrumb path 68
Breadcrumbs 215
Breadcrumb trail. *See* Breadcrumbs
bulletin board 170

C

CachedViewModes setting 217
caching system
  about 213, 214
  advanced settings 224
  default settings 223
  settings, customizing 228, 229
  template cache 214
  template, compiling 216
  template, optimization 216
  view cache 216
caching system, advanced settings
  about 224
  opcode cache 226, 227
  override cache 224
  pre-generation cache 224
  proxy and HTTP accelerator 227
  role cache 225
  static cache 225, 226
  translation cache 225
caching system, default settings
  about 223
  NodeTreeCaching 223
  TemplateCompile 223
  TemplateCompression 223
  TemplateOptimization 223
  ViewCaching 223
children, content class
  sorting, by default 57
class attributes
  about 52

elements 52
translating 187-189
class attributes, elements
  datatype-specific controls 52
  generic control 52, 53
  internal identifier 52
  name 52, 53
classes/, extension directory structure 91
class templates
  issue archive template 152
  issue article template 157
  issue template 146
  issue year template 155
  staff profile template 140
ClearCacheMethod, smart cache 222
ClearRelationTypes setting 219
CMF 10
code debugger
  about 253
  debug template, operators 254
conditional control, control structure operator
  about 108, 109
  IF-THEN-ELSE 108, 109
container checkbox, content class 57
content
  and design, separating 50
  comanaging 49, 50
  object-oriented content 50, 51
  structure, in eZ Publish 50
  translating 190
content area, content structure
  about 71, 72
  details 72
  locations 73
  object contextual menu 74
  preview 72
  relations 73
  sub items 74
  translations 72
content class package
  about 99
  creating, steps 99-103
Content Management Framework. *See* CMF
content object 50
ContentSettings
  CachedViewModes setting 217

content structure, backend
  about 69
  content area 71, 72
  secondary menu 70
content template 129
content tree 75, 76
  about 75
  article, creating 85
  feedback form 87
  other sections 88
  staff section 83, 85
control structure operator, templating
      markup
  conditional control 108, 109
  loop control 109
Cronjob, extension 90
cronjobs/, extension directory structure 91
CSS
  classes-colors.css 124
  content.css 124
  core.css 124
  editing 124
  pagelayout.css 124
  site-colors.css 124
  webstyletoolbar.css 124
custom template file, override system
  creating 140

D

database, eZ Publish site
  code, deploying 241
  deploying 241
  extension, configuring 241, 242
  files, excluding from deploy 242
  synchronization, starting 243
Data Import extension 261
datatype, extension 90
datatypes 53
datatypes/, extension directory structure 91
datetime() operator 109
debug-accumulator operator 255
debug-log operator 254
debug template, operators
  debug-accumulator 255
  debug-log 254
  debug-timing-point 254

debug-timing-point operator 254
DependentClassIdentifier, smart cache 221
design activation, extension 98
design, creating
  about 113
  homepage 114
  issue archive page 116
  issue page 115
  staff profile page 116, 117
design extension
  about 90
  creating, steps 92, 93
design/, extension directory structure 91
dev
  site accesses, creating for 41
developing siteaccess 38
development environment 232

E

ECM 9
Enterprise content management. *See* ECM
Enterprise Content Management System 9
enterprise siteaccess schema, siteaccess
      system
  dev 41
  dev_panel 41
  staging 41
  staging_panel 41
environment
  about 231
  development environment 232
  eproduction environment 232, 233
  staging environment 232
eventtypes/, extension directory structure 91
expiry parameter 214
extension
  about 89
  building 91
  directory structure 90
  distributing, ways 105
  folder structure 193
  packtmedia extension, building 91
  siteaccess 193
  types 90
extension, activating
  about 96

backend activation 97, 98
design activation 98
manually 96, 97
extension, building
designing 92, 93
settings 92
template operator extension 94
translation extension 94, 95
extension, directory structure
actions/ 91
autoloads/ 91
bin/ 91
classes/ 91
cronjobs/ 91
datatypes/ 91
design/ 91
eventtypes/ 91
modules/ 91
packages/ 91
settings/ 91
translations/ 91
extension package
creating 103, 104
extension, portability
about 99
content class package 99
content class package, creating 99-103
packages, creating 103, 104
extension, types
bin 90
Cronjob 90
datatype 90
design 90
fetch function 90
module 90
operator 90
translation 90
workflow event 90
eZ CMF 10
eZ components
about 10, 15
CMF 10
installing 15
making available 15
eZ Deploy 261
eZ Deploy, eZ Publish site 234
eZ Flow 11, 12

eZ JSCore extension 260
eZ Publish
about 9, 10
Apache virtual host, settings 17, 18, 36
backend 68, 69
configuration files 21, 22
content class 52
content structure 50
Cron jobs 20
database, initializing 16, 17
datatypes 53
default configuration settings 39
extension 89
features 10
hosting 12
image host, settings 20
installation 12
installation, unpacking 16
internationalization 184
[IP_ADDRESS], variable 19
locale file, creating 184, 185
locale identifier 184
localization 184
multi-language sites management 186
NameVirtualHost setting 19
[PATH_TO_EZPUBLISH], variable 19
[PORT], variable 19
[SERVER_ALIAS], variable 19
[SERVER_NAME], variable 19
setting up 16
setup wizard 22
siteaccess system 37, 38
templating 107
translations.ts file 185, 186
eZ Publish content class
about 52
class attributes 52, 53
management 54, 55
references 55
structure 56
eZ Publish content class, structure
attributes 58
children sorting, by default 57
identifier property 57
name property 57
object name pattern 57
URL alias name pattern 57

eZ Publish, extensions
  about 259
  Data Import extension 261
  eZ Deploy extension 261
  eZ JSCore 260
  eZ Publish OE extension 260
  eZ Xajax 259
  Google Sitemaps extension 260
  Star Rating 259, 260
eZ Publish, installation
  eZ components 15
  hardware, requisites 13
  hosting, requisites 12
  PHP configuration 13
  shared versus dedicated host 14
  software, requisites 12
eZ Publish OE extension 260
eZ Publish Online Editor. *See* **eZ Publish OE extension**
eZ Publish, packages
  about 10
  eZ Flow 11, 12
  eZ Webin 11
  Plain Site 11
eZ Publish site, deploying
  about 233, 234
  automatic tests, creating 234, 235
  database, deploying 241
  eZ Deploy 234
  production server, deploying on 245
  production siteaccesses, configuring 240
  quality assurance 245
  staging siteaccesses, configuring 240
  validity, checking 243, 244
ezstring attribute 141
ezwebin
  about 117
  forum, adding 168, 169
  new section, creating 118-120
  page layout, customizing 123, 124
  predefined groups 204
  project, section for 118
  section permission access, setting up 120-123
  standard page layout, overriding 118
eZ Webin 11
ezwebin cache block, template cache 215

ezwebin, predefined groups
  administrator users 204
  anonymous users 204
  editors 204
  members 204
  partners 204
eZ Xajax extension 259

F

feed
  adding, to site 175
  blog feed, creating 176-178
  feed source, configuring 178
  forum feed, creating 180, 181
  multisource feed 181
  setting up 175
feedback form, content tree 87, 88
fetch_alias function 163
fetch function, extension 90
fetch functions, templating markup 109
file_update_protection parameter 250
folders, issue archive section
  adding 82, 83
forum access control list 170
forum, adding
  forum access control list 170
  Private forums section, creating 171-173
  steps 168, 169
  sticky post, creating 170
forum feed
  creating 180, 181

G

GD2 20
generic control, class attribute
  about 53
  information collector 53
  required 53
  searchable 53
  translatable 53
Google Sitemaps extension 260

H

has_access_to fetch function 164
host

used, for siteaccess selecting 47
hosting, eZ Publish
  PHP configuration 13
  requisites 12
  software, requisites 12

I

i18n. *See* internationalization
i18n operator 194
identifier, content class 57
ignore_content_expiry parameter 214
image_class parameter 142
ImageMagick 20
information collector 53
installing, APC
  from sources 249
  PECL used 249
  steps 248, 249
Integration platform environment 231
Internationalization 184
issue archive section, content tree
  object, editing 76-80
issue archive template, class templates
  embed template 155
  full template 153, 154
issue article template, class templates
  $versionview_mode variable 163
  embed template 165
  ezini operator 162
  fetch_alias function 163
  full template 159-165
  has_access_to fetch function 164
  line template 157
  SummaryInFullView parameter 162
  tipafriend function 164
issue template, class templates
  about 146
  {attribute_view_gui attribute=$node.data_
      map. short_description} function 147
  authors.tpl template 147
  embed template 152
  full template 148, 149, 150
  line template 146
  parent_node_id parameter 150
  thumb template 151
  uri parameter 147

issue year template, class templates
  full template 156, 157

K

keys parameter 214
Klingonian locale file 185

L

l10n operator 194
L10n. *See* localization
lastname object attribute 142
left menu 70
locale identifier
  about 184
  new locale file, creating 184, 185
  translations.ts file 185, 186
localization 184
login handler, extension 90
loop control, control structure operator
  about 109
  FOR-FOREACH-WHILE 109

M

magazine's blog
  blog, adding to site 174
  creating 173
magazine's forum
  forum, adding 168, 169
manual activation, extension 96
MaxParents, smart cache 222
module, extension 90
modules/, extension directory structure 91
multi-language sites, management
  about 186
  class attributes, translating 187-189
  class default language 190
  content, translating 190
  URL, translating 191, 192
multilingual extensions
  extension folder, structure 192, 193
  siteaccess 193
  template strings 194
multilingual siteaccesses
  configuration file, copying 44
  creating 44

ini files, editing for locale components 44, 45
multiplexer event, workflow event 205
multisource feed 181

N

name, class attribute 52, 53
name property, content class 57
news feed. *See* feed
node 51
node system template 129
NodeTreeCaching setting 223
notification workflow
  creating 206-211

O

ObjectFilter, smart cache 222
object, issue archive section
  editing 76-80
  HTML embedding, inside WYSIWYG XML editor 81
  short description 80, 81
  show children checkbox 82
  tags input 82
object name pattern, content class 57
object-oriented content 50, 51
OmniGraffle 113
opcode cache 226, 227
operator, extension 90
operators, templating markup 110
override cache 224
override system
  about 130
  custom template file, creating 140
  template override. creating 130, 131
  template override. creating from graphic interfaces 131-134
  template override, creating manually 134

P

packages/, extension directory structure 91
Packt Media Sites, content class
  attributes 58
  profile content class, creating 59-61

page layout
  about 113
  homepage 114
  issue archive page 116
  issue page 115
  staff profile page 116, 117
page layout, ezwebin
  CSS, editing 124
  customizing 123, 124
  new style package, creating 124-128
parent_node_id parameter 150
payment event, workflow event 206
PECL
  used, for installing APC 249
Pencil 113
PHP configuration, eZ Publish installation
  PHP memory limit issue 13
  PHP timezone 13
PHPOperatorList array key 142
PHPUnit 235
Plain Site 11
policies 196
pre-generation cache 224
Private forums section
  creating 171-173
production environment
  about 232, 233
  preparing 233
production siteaccesses
  configuring 240
profile content class, Packt Media Site
  Article class, extending 63, 64
  creating 59, 60, 61, 62, 63
  other content classes 65

Q

QT technical documentation site
  URL 185

R

RelatedSiteAccessList setting 218
role cache 225
roles
  about 196
  applying 196

S

Selenium 235
Selenium IDE
  about 236
  installing 236
  session, recording 236, 237, 238
Selenium Integrated Development Environment. *See* **Selenium IDE**
settings/, extension directory structure 91
setup wizard, eZ Publish
  about 23
  database, initialization 27
  database, selecting 26
  email, settings 25
  finishing 36
  language support 28
  site access, configuration 32, 33
  site, details 33, 34
  site, packages 29, 30, 31
  site, registration 35
  site, security 34
  system check 23, 24
shared
  versus dedicated hosting 14
shorten operator 142
simple shipping event, workflow event 205
siteaccesses, selecting
  default siteaccess, setting 46
  host-based matching used 47
  URI-based matching used 46
siteaccess folder structure
  about 39
  admin folder 40
  default configuration settings 39, 40
  ezwebin_site folder 40
  global overrides 39
  ita. eng. fre folder 40
  setup folder 40
  siteaccess, creating for dev 40
  siteaccess settings 39, 40
SiteAccessSettings
  RelatedSiteAccessList setting 218
siteaccess system
  about 37, 38
  creating, for dev 40, 41
  creating, for staging 42

  database parameters, configuring 43, 44
  developing siteaccess 38
  enterprise site access schema 41
  eZ Publish documentation, scenario 38
  public interface 37
  restricted interface 37
  siteaccess folder structure 39, 40
  staging siteaccess 38
  symbolic links, creating 42, 43
smart cache
  about 220
  AdditionalObjectIDs 222
  ClearCacheMethod 222
  DependentClassIdentifier 221
  disabling 220
  enabling 220
  MaxParents 222
  ObjectFilter 222
SmartCacheClear setting 220
Smarty
  URL 107
staff profile template, class templates
  $node 141
  $node.data_map attribute 141
  $node.data_map.profile_description.content.output.output_text attribute 142
  $node.name attribute 141
  $node.object.data_map attribute 141
  $node.url_alias attribute 141
  about 140
  alignment 142
  attribute_view_gui function 141
  css_class parameter 142
  embed remplate 146
  ezstring attribute 141
  full template 143, 144, 145
  image_class parameter 142
  lastname object attribute 142
  line template 140
  PHPOperatorList array key 142
  shorten operator 142
staff section, content tree
  about 83
  Create here button 83
  Profile edit page 85
  Profile voice 83
  The staff node 83

staging
  site accesses, creating for 41
staging environment 232
staging siteaccess 38
staging siteaccesses
  configuring 240
standard page layout, ezwebin
  new section, creating 118-120
  overriding 118
  project, section for 118
  section permission access, setting up 120-
    123
Star Rating extension 259, 260
static cache 225, 226
subtree_expiry parameter 214
SummaryInFullView parameter 162

T

template
  tips 229, 230
template cache, caching system
  ezwebin cache block 215
template cache. caching system
  about 214
  cache keys 214
  content expiration 214
  expiry parameter 214
  ignore_content_expiry parameter 214
  keys parameter 214
  subtree expiration 214
  subtree_expiry parameter 214
  time-based expiration 214
TemplateCache setting 215, 223
template, caching system
  compiling 216
  optimization 216
template compile, caching system
  about 216
  TemplateOptimization configuration 216
TemplateCompile configuration 216
TemplateCompile setting 223
TemplateCompile settings 216
TemplateCompression setting 223
template debugger
  about 255
  enabling 256

ShowXHTMLCode, enabling 257
  verbose debug output enabling, Debug
    parameter used 257
template functions, templating markup
  $classification variable 112
  about 110
  HTML, embedding inside WYSIWYG XML
    Editor pt.2 111, 112
  layout variables 111
  template, overriding 111
template operator extension 94
Template Operator extension 91
TemplateOptimization configuration 216
TemplateOptimization setting 223
template override
  creating 130, 131
  creating, from graphic interfaces 131-134
  creating, manually 134
template override, manual creation
  article class 138
  folder class, for issue 136, 137
  folder class, for issue archive section 138
  folder class, for issue year archive 136
  frontpage embed object 139
  profile class 135, 136
TemplateSettings
  TemplateCache setting 215
  TemplateCompile settings 216
template, types
  content template 129
  node system template 129
templating, eZ Publish
  about 107
  markup 108
templating markup, eZ Publish
  about 108
  control structure operator 108
  fetch functions 109
  operators 110
  template functions 110
thread 170
tipafriend function 164
translation cache 225
translation extension 90, 94, 95
translations/, extension directory structure
  91
translations.ts file 185, 186

U

URI
  used, for siteaccess selecting 46
uri parameter 147
URL
  translating 191, 192
URL alias name pattern, content class 57
user
  accounts 198, 199
  classes, extending 202
  creating 199-201
  deleting 203, 204
  disabling 202, 203
  managing 202
user group 197
user management
  about 202
  eZ Publish user classes, extending 202
  new user, creating 199, 201
  user accounts 198, 199
  user, deleting 203, 204
  user, disabling 202, 203

V

view cache, caching system
  about 216, 217
  cache by context, disabling 217
  cache by context. enabling 217
  CachedViewModes setting 217
  clearing 218, 219
  disabling 217
  enabling 217
  smart cache 220-222
ViewCacheSettings
  ClearRelationTypes setting 219
  SmartCacheClear setting 220
ViewCaching setting 223
Virtual Private Server. *See* VPS
VPS 14

W

wait until date event, workflow event 205
wireframe editors 113
workflow
  about 204

default workflow events 205
  notification workflow, creating 206-211
workflow event, extension 90
workflow events (default)
  approve event 205
  multiplexer event 205
  payment gateway event 206
  simple shipping event 205
  wait until date event 205

X

XPath 239

[PACKT] PUBLISHING
Thank you for buying
eZ Publish 4: Enterprise Web Sites Step-by-Step

Packt Open Source Project Royalties

When we sell a book written on an Open Source project, we pay a royalty directly to that project. Therefore by purchasing eZ Publish 4: Enterprise Web Sites Step-by-Step, Packt will have given some of the money received to the eZ Publish project.

In the long term, we see ourselves and you—customers and readers of our books—as part of the Open Source ecosystem, providing sustainable revenue for the projects we publish on. Our aim at Packt is to establish publishing royalties as an essential part of the service and support a business model that sustains Open Source.

If you're working with an Open Source project that you would like us to publish on, and subsequently pay royalties to, please get in touch with us.

Writing for Packt

We welcome all inquiries from people who are interested in authoring. Book proposals should be sent to author@packtpub.com. If your book idea is still at an early stage and you would like to discuss it first before writing a formal book proposal, contact us; one of our commissioning editors will get in touch with you.

We're not just looking for published authors; if you have strong technical skills but no writing experience, our experienced editors can help you develop a writing career, or simply get some additional reward for your expertise.

About Packt Publishing

Packt, pronounced 'packed', published its first book "Mastering phpMyAdmin for Effective MySQL Management" in April 2004 and subsequently continued to specialize in publishing highly focused books on specific technologies and solutions.

Our books and publications share the experiences of your fellow IT professionals in adapting and customizing today's systems, applications, and frameworks. Our solution-based books give you the knowledge and power to customize the software and technologies you're using to get the job done. Packt books are more specific and less general than the IT books you have seen in the past. Our unique business model allows us to bring you more focused information, giving you more of what you need to know, and less of what you don't.

Packt is a modern, yet unique publishing company, which focuses on producing quality, cutting-edge books for communities of developers, administrators, and newbies alike. For more information, please visit our website: www.PacktPub.com.

PHP 5 CMS Framework Development

ISBN: 978-1-847193-57-5   Paperback: 348 pages

Expert insight and practical guidance to creating an efficient, flexible, and robust framework for a PHP 5-based content management system

1. Learn how to design, build, and implement a complete CMS framework for your custom requirements

2. Implement a solid architecture with object orientation, MVC

3. Build an infrastructure for custom menus, modules, components, sessions, user tracking, and more

MODx Web Development

ISBN: 978-1-847194-90-9   Paperback: 276 pages

Building dynamic websites with the PHP application framework and CMS

1. Simple, step-by-step instructions detailing how to install, configure, and customize MODx

2. Covers detailed theory from the basics, to practical implementation

3. Learn the most common web requirements and solutions, and build a site in the process

Please check **www.PacktPub.com** for information on our titles

Managing eZ Publish Web Content Management Projects

ISBN: 978-1-847191-72-4   Paperback: 320 pages

Strategies, best practices, and techniques for implementing eZ publish open-source CMS projects to delight your clients

1. Tips and expert advice for the whole eZ publish web CMS project lifecycle

2. Learn about the requirements and success factors of an eZ project

3. Implement eZ publish projects successfully, efficiently, and effectively

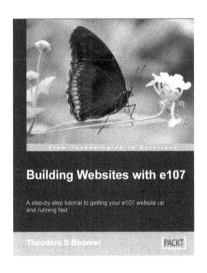

Building Websites with e107

ISBN: 978-1-904811-31-2   Paperback: 260 pages

A step by step tutorial to getting your e107 website up and running fast

1. Get your e107 website up fast

2. Simple and practical guide to mastering e107

3. Customize and extend your e107 site with new templates and the CMS plug-in

Please check **www.PacktPub.com** for information on our titles

www.ingramcontent.com/pod-product-compliance
Lightning Source LLC
Chambersburg PA
CBHW060520060326
40690CB00017B/3332